The ABC's of Bible Study

by

Gary Edwin Ford

Available from:
Advent*Source*
5040 Prescott Avenue
Lincoln, NE 68506
800-328-0525
www.adventsource.org

ISBN# 1-57756-411-1

Printed in the United Stated of America

Table of Contents

1. **The ABC's of Bible Study------------------ 1**

2. **The Divinity of Jesus----------------------- 9**

3. **Death---21**

4. **Heaven ---------------------------------------57**

5. **The Rapture --------------------------------67**

6. **Hell --97**

7. **Baptism------------------------------------ 115**

8. **Saturday or Sunday? -------------------- 125**
    1. First Day Texts **128**
    2. The Lord's Day: is it Saturday or Sunday?..... **139**
    3. The Resurrection Memorial **142**
    4. Does God's Law Change? **143**
    5. The New Testament Day of Worship **175**
    6. Is Sabbath-keeping Jewish? **182**
    7. Which Day is God's Sabbath Today? **186**

9. **Does It Really Matter? ------------------ 193**

Appendix ----------------------------------- 203

Scriptural Index -------------------------- 206

Topical Index ------------------------------ 224

Abreviations ------------------------------- 225

The following people played a special and significant part in helping to make this book a reality. To them I am deeply indebted:

My wife, Yvonne R. Ford
Dr. Robert Nutter
Elder John DuNesme
My mother, Laura Mae Ford

When reading the King James version of the Bible, you will notice that some words are *italicized.* The translators of the King James Version put words in *italics* when they were not in the original manuscripts, but rather supplied by the translators to help clarify the meaning of the verse.

In my book, *italics* are used, just as the writers of the King James Bible wrote them. Words in **bold** are my emphasis.

It is my prayer that this book be used as a tool to increase the Kingdom of God and further the teachings of Jesus as stated in Matthew 28:19-20:

> Go ye therefore, and teach all nations, baptizing them in the name of the Father, and of the Son, and of the Holy Ghost: teaching them to observe all things whatsoever I have commanded you, and, lo, I am with you alway, even unto the end of the world. Amen.

The ABC's of Bible Study

In Christianity alone there are over 300 denominations, all claiming to have the truth and each one claiming that the other religions are wrong. Ten Christians of different faiths can read the same verses from the same source, the Bible, and come up with ten different doctrines about the same subject.

What is an honest Christian to believe?

Today, on the subject of the second coming of Jesus, the teachings are so varied that you would think different Christians are waiting for different events to take place, yet all are quoting the same verses but in different ways. Confused? No wonder! Up until now there has been almost nothing on the market to help searching Christians find answers for themselves. There are many books propounding one teaching over another but almost nothing to help the sincere Christian compare the facts, with the help of the Holy Spirit, in the quiet of the home, to find what God really has so say about the different subjects of the Bible.

The purpose of this book, therefore, is to give to the sincere Christian the tools to work with in order to rightly divide the Word of Truth (2 Timothy 2:15). It is called the ABC's of Bible Study.

A = Assumption that God does not lie

B = Big Picture

C = Context

A = Assume God does not lie.

This may sound oversimplified, but think about it. Does God teach two different doctrines, so contradictory that if you believe one doctrine is truth, you have to believe that the other one is false? This makes God look foolish and it's as if He is a liar. So the first assumption that the sincere Christian must start with is that God is not the one who is confused and lying to us by saying one thing in one place and then changing His mind in the next book of the Bible and saying the opposite is true. Note the following verses that back up this principle.

Numb. 23:19	"God *is* not a man, that he should lie…"
Mal. 3:6	"For I *am* the Lord, I change not…"
Jn. 10:35	"…the scripture **cannot** be broken."
2 Tim. 2:13	"…he **cannot** deny himself."
Titus 1:2	"…God, that cannot lie…"
Heb. 6:18	"*it was* impossible for God to lie..."
Heb. 13:8	"Jesus Christ **the same** yesterday, and today, and forever."
James 1:17	"Every good gift and every perfect gift is from above, and cometh down from the father of lights, with whom is **no variableness**, neither shadow of turning."

A Assumption that God does not lie or contradict Himself.

In each chapter, we will consider some of the implications of contradictory viewpoints and show that if we assume God does not lie, it means that one view is true and the remaining view must be false. Sometimes a certain view or doctrine carries with it overtones and implications not always realized or meant by those advocating that teaching. I will try to bring out those implications in the first part of every chapter under the "A" for the **assumption** that God does not lie.

B = Big Picture

Soon after sincere Christians begin the study of God's Word, they find what **appears to be** gross contradictions about certain subjects, that make a clear-cut answer next to impossible without taking a denominational bias in one way or another.

The Bible claims to be inspired by God (2 Pet. 1:20-21). If that is true, which I believe it is, then it cannot contradict itself in its teachings. If it **appears to contradict**, then I must not understand it correctly. In Isa. 28:10 we are told to line up texts, compare them and the ideas that they present, and thereby arrive at truth; it also helps us to understand where false teachings get their start.

In the study of almost any subject of the Bible, there are verses that **appear**, at first glance, to contradict each other and cause confusion. If there are fifteen verses on any one subject of the Bible, you will find, for example, that twelve out of fifteen (the majority) will point towards one teaching and the remaining three (minority) will **appear** to point towards a completely different teaching. If we line up the verses on any one given subject, in diagram form, it will look like this:

TRUTH

ERROR

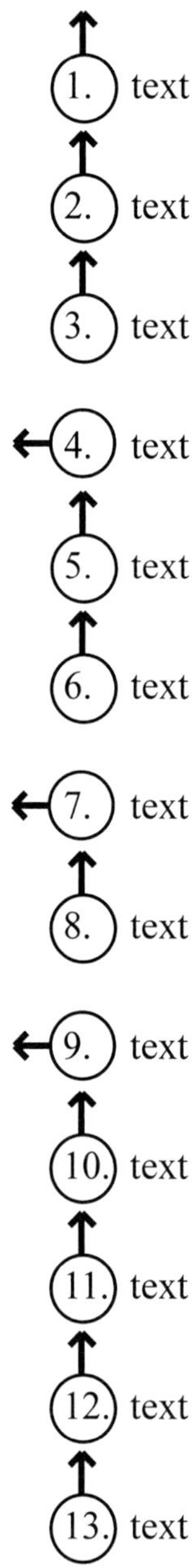

Many erroneous teachings are based on one to three texts of the Bible, while the majority of the texts on the same subject are ignored, and error is taught in the place of truth.

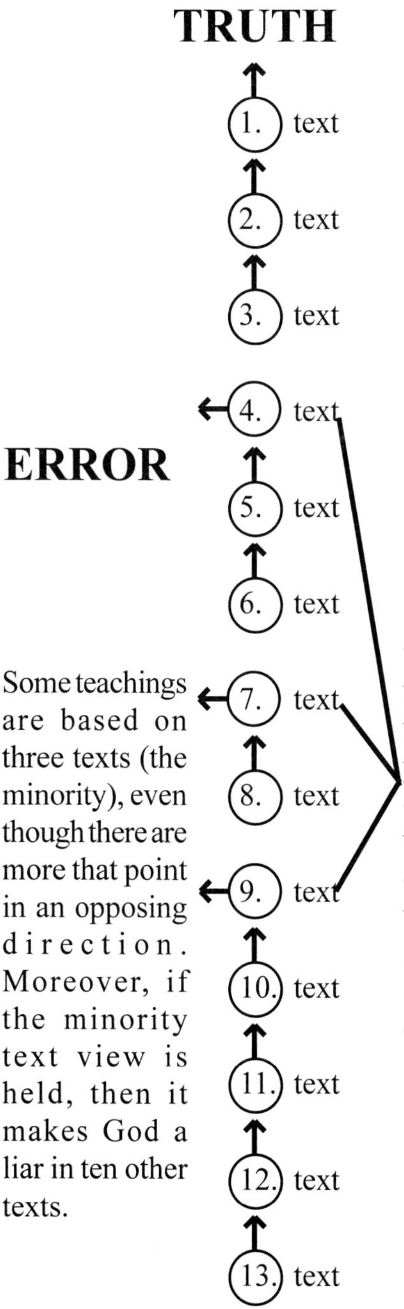

Build your beliefs on the majority of the texts.

Some teachings are based on three texts (the minority), even though there are more that point in an opposing direction. Moreover, if the minority text view is held, then it makes God a liar in ten other texts.

When we study the context surrounding these texts, we find that they **only appear** to point in an opposing direction. In reality, they point in the same direction as the other ten verses and give support to our original assumption that **God does not lie.**

After studying carefully the context of the three or four verses that **appear to be contradictory**, you will find that they line up with the rest of the twelve, and all say the same thing. This shows that God does not lie and teach two opposing views, but indicates only one as truth. So, "B" stands for the **Big Picture**.

C = Context

We must always consider the context of Biblical verses in order not to twist a verse to make it say something that the original writer did not have in mind. There are two areas of context to consider as one studies the Bible for truth.

1. Literary context
2. Historical context

Literary context: It is always important to read the verses before and after the verse you are studying to make sure that you are **rightly dividing** the original writer's intent.

Historical context: Many times modern-day Christians get confused with their Biblical understanding when they put a twenty first-century understanding upon a word or phrase that did not have that meaning or intent back in the first century when it was written or in the seventeenth century when it was first translated into English.

The Bible is a book written, for the most part, by Hebrew authors and shows God's dealing with mankind through the Jewish nation. We must take this into consideration as we rightly divide the Word of Truth, so as not to twist the meaning of a verse and end up with an incorrect doctrine.

All doctrine derived from the Bible should be in agreement with the way the Bible authors themselves used a word or phrase. Therefore, the careful student will not take liberties to use any phrase of the Bible for private interpretation (2 Pet. 1:20). Thus, "C" stands for **context**.

Some people assume that because the King James Version of the Bible has been around longer it is more accurate. Actually the opposite is true. Since the printing of the King James Version in 1611, many new manuscripts have been discovered by archaeologists that shed light on some of the difficult passages of the Scriptures. So, **just because a translation is older does not mean that it is necessarily more sacred or accurate.** You can find **truth** from any translation of the Bible, but for the most part I have used the King James Version because it is so widely used.

Some of the other translations that I quote from will be abbreviated as follows:

NEB = New English Bible
NAB = New American Bible
RSV = Revised Standard Version
NIV = New International Version

Review

A = Assumption that God does not lie

B = Big Picture

C = Context

Let us apply these three simple ABC's to a Bible doctrine now and see how they work in helping us to **rightly divide** the Word of Truth (2 Tim. 2:15).

If we diagram our findings, it will look like this:

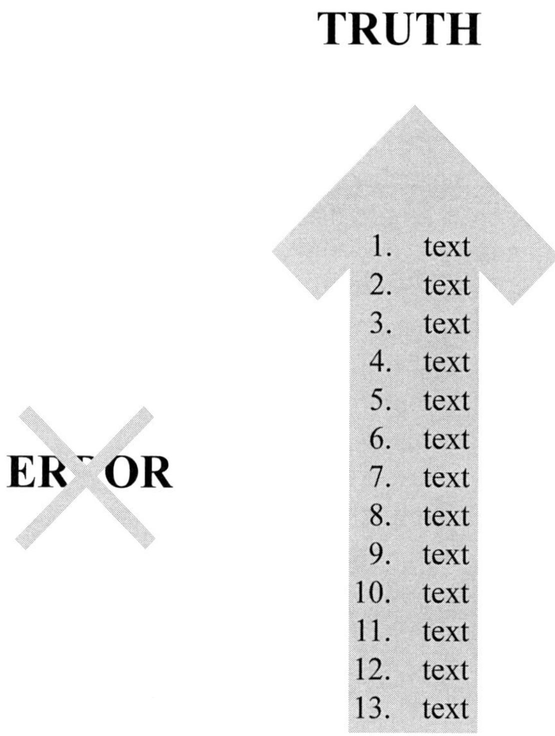

The Divinity of Jesus

Most churches today teach the divinity of Jesus. Jesus is part of the Trinity, the second person of the Godhead, equal with the Father, always has been God, and **is not** a created being. Listed below are the main verses that have a bearing on the divinity of Jesus. Notice that most of the verses point toward one conclusion. That conclusion is easily distinguishable as the Big Picture or the "B" of our ABC's. Notice the three verses that **appear at first glance** to point in another direction.

Carefully check the list with your own Bible and compare the texts. I have underlined key parts of the different verses and left out some parts of verses in the interest of condensing and saving space. If you feel that I have left out a verse that will shed more light on this subject, then add it to your list and continue to compare Scripture with Scripture.

If the "A" of the ABC's is correct, then God cannot be backing both views. The two contradictory views are listed below. Note them carefully.

1. **Jesus is part of the Trinity, equal to the Father and not a created being.**

2. **Jesus is a created being, not equal to the Father.**

Let us look at the Big Picture, and compare texts.

Jesus is fully divine, equal to the Father, part of the Trinity.

↑

(1.) **Isa. 9:6** "For unto us a child is born...and his name shall be called Wonderful, Counsellor, The mighty God, The everlasting Father, The Prince of Peace."

↑

(2.) **Micah 5:2** "But thou, Bethlehem...out of thee shall he come forth unto me...whose goings forth *have been* from of old, **from everlasting**."

↑

(3.) **Jn. 1:1-3, 10, 14** "...the Word **was** God....All things were made by him...He was in the world... and the world knew him not.... And the Word was made flesh, and dwelt among us..."

↑

(4.) **Jn. 5:17,18** "...My Father worketh hitherto, and I work. Therefore the Jews sought the more to kill him, because he... said also that God was his Father, making himself **equal** with God.

Jesus is a created being; not divine and not equal to the Father.

Jesus is fully divine, equal to the Father, part of the Trinity.

5. **Jn. 8:56-59** "Your father Abraham rejoiced to see my day; and he *saw it* and was glad....Thou art not yet fifty years old, and hast thou seen Abraham? Jesus said... before Abraham was, **I Am.**"

6. **Jn. 10:30, 33** **"I and my Father are one**. Then the Jews took up stones again to stone him... saying...**because that thou, being a man, makest thyself God**."

Jesus is a created being; not divine and not equal to the Father.

7. **Jn. 14:28** "...my Father is greater than I."

8. **Jn. 17:5** "...glorify thou me...with the glory which I had with thee before the world was."

9. **Eph. 3:9** "...which from the beginning of the world hath been hid in God, who created all things by Jesus Christ."

Jesus is fully divine, equal to the Father, part of the Trinity.

↑

(10.) **Phil. 2:5-8** "...Christ Jesus: Who, being in the form of God, **thought it not robbery** to be **equal** with God..."

Jesus is a created being; not divine and not equal to the Father. ←

(11.) **Col. 1:14-16** "In whom we have redemption through his blood... Who is the image of the invisible God, **The firstborn** of every creature: For **by him were all things created**...all things were created by him, and for him."

↑

(12.) **Heb. 1:2** (God) "Hath...spoken unto us by *his* Son, whom he hath appointed heir of all things, by whom also **he made** the worlds."

← (13.) **Rev. 3:14** "...These things saith the Amen, the faithful and true witness, **the beginning** of the creation of God."

There are three verses that **appear** to be out of line with the Big Picture, so let us examine them carefully (looking at their context) to see if they truly contradict the other ten verses.

Text #7 **Jn. 14:28** "...my Father is greater than I."

The only time that the Father was greater than the Son was while Jesus was on this earth and had the limitations of a human body. While He was in human form, He did not have the form of God, and that was by choice. TEXT #10 on our list says that before Christ was human, **He "thought it not robbery to be equal with God:** But made himself of no reputation and took upon him the form of a servant, and was made in the likeness of men..." So before He was born on this earth, **He was equal with God**.

This tells us that the only thing that Jesus was saying when He spoke the words, "My Father is greater than I," is that while He was in human form, He was not using His own divine power, but the Father's (Jn. 5:19, 30), and He was not in the form of God, but voluntarily restricted to the limitations of His human body, thus making the Father greater.

Other than being restricted voluntarily by not using His divine power while in the form of a human, our text does not indicate that Jesus was any less God while He was human. We know that He was sinless (1 Pet. 2:22) and perfect in every way, giving us a good example of how a human can walk in the Spirit, according to the will of God.

Text #11 **Col. 1:14-16** "In whom we have redemption through his blood...Who is the image of the invisible God, the firstborn of every creature: For by him were all things created...all things were created by him, and for him."

The difficult phrase in this verse is the one that refers to Christ as "**the firstborn** of every creature." Does this phrase mean that Christ was the first creature created by the Father and therefore a created being? **If** this were the intent of the original writer, this verse teaches something that is contradictory to the other ten verses that teach Jesus is divine and **not** a created being.

The word **firstborn** in the Greek is "prototokos." This word is used elsewhere referring to Christ. In Heb. 1:6 "prototokos" is used, but clearly refers to the incarnation. Some have tried the same application here in Col. 1:15, but it really does not fit. Others believe Paul is referring to the resurrection of the dead. However, neither interpretation fits the context. Christ is here presented as the Creator (Col. 1:16) and as preceding creation (Jn. 1:1-3, 10, 14).

The passage (Col. 1:16) may be understood in harmony with the Big Picture, painted by so many other verses in the Bible. To make Christ first in rank, as **head of the human family**, would make Christ's position unique, authoritative and absolute. He is the head of a royal family, as in the human sense, someone who would be called the firstborn. The firstborn in a human setting is the one that **ranks first** among all the children. Therefore, Paul uses the term to denote Christ as the one who is first in rank. When this verse is understood this way, it does not say that Christ was a created being **but instead that He is the head of the human family.**

The Bible clearly teaches that Satan is the father of lies (Jn. 8:44), and that God is not the author of confusion, but of order (1 Cor. 14:33, 40). Let us keep in mind our original assumption that God does not lie and contradict Himself. That assumption will help us to know how to understand some of the difficult verses of the Bible. We will know in advance which way to understand them from the way the Big Picture looks on our chart.

Text #13 **Rev. 3:14** "...These things saith the Amen, the faithful and true witness, the beginning of the creation of God."

This text refers to Jesus as the **Amen** and **the true and faithful witness**, but then says, "**the beginning** of the creation of God." The last part definitely gives the reader the impression that Jesus is a created being. However, when it is examined closely, we find that it too can be understood in two very different ways. One makes God a liar, contradicting Himself, and the other is in harmony with the plain Biblical teaching that Jesus is divine, equal to the Father.

The difficult phrase in the passage is "**the beginning** of the creation of God." The word **"beginning"** in the Greek is "arche." This word was used in the active or passive voice with slightly different meanings. If it is taken passively, it means that Jesus was the first thing acted upon, or, in other words, that Christ was the first being that was created. But if it is taken actively, then it means that Christ was the Creator, or Prime Mover, who initiated the first act of creation. If we look over the verses that we have listed in our original chart, it is easy to see that **Christ is mentioned as the Creator** in the following texts:

Text #3 "All things were made by him..."

Text #3 "...the world was made by him..."

Text #9 "...who created all things by Jesus Christ."

Text #11 "...for by him were all things created..."

Text #12 "...Son...by whom also he made the worlds..."

Understanding the Greek word in the active sense would make Jesus the Creator who "spake and it was *done*; he commanded, and it stood fast" (Psm. 33:6, 9). This would harmonize with the Big Picture that the Bible paints about the divinity of Jesus.

Now we understand how some cults teach that Jesus is not part of the Trinity. They base their entire doctrine on three texts, which, at first glance, appear to say that Jesus is a created being.

Too often men build a doctrine on one or two texts that **appear to be** in contradiction with the Biblical context and the Big Picture. This is why we have so many different denominations and doctrines from one book. Many times this building of doctrines on the minority of texts causes the sincere Bible student to be left in confusion and bewilderment, wondering what to believe.

In Nehemiah 9:6-15 it says the Lord did all of the following things:

(verse 6) made heaven and earth

(verse 7) chose Abraham

(verses 9-11) delivered Israel from Pharaoh in Egypt

(verse 13) gave the Ten Commandments from Mt. Sinai

(verse 15) gave them bread and water from the rock

In 1 Cor. 10:1-4 it clearly states that the Rock was **Christ**. Therefore Christ is identified as being **the Lord** who was responsible for all the aformentioned acts: creator, friend of Abraham, deliverer of Israel from Egypt, and the giver of the Ten Commandments. The Bible says the Ten Commandments were written by the finger of God (Ex. 31:18). According to what Paul says in 1 Cor. 10:4, that was the finger of Christ, who **is** the Creator and God of the Old Testament. Note the following verses that back up this conclusion and fit with the Big Picture. James 4:12 says, "There is **one lawgiver,** who is able to save and destroy." And Acts 4:10-12 says that the Saviour is Jesus Christ of Nazareth. When Jesus claimed the title of the **I Am** in John 8:56-59 (TEXT # 5), the people wanted to stone Him. Why? Because that is the name that God used as He dealt with Moses from the burning bush (Ex. 3:13-14). No wonder the Jews wanted to stone Jesus! He was claiming to be the God that spoke to Moses from the burning bush in the O.T.!

There are many verses in the Bible that identify Jesus as the Creator, being fully divine, equal to the Father and **not a created being**. Notice the verses that refer to God in a plural form, indicating more than one and backing up the idea of the Trinity: Gen. 1:26; 3:22, 11:7 and Isa. 6:8.

If you take just a moment to look up **all** of the texts on the divinity of Jesus, you will find perfect harmony in the Word of God on this subject.

ASK YOURSELF

1. Does the Bible ever put Jesus in the same list with the Father and the Holy Spirit (Mt. 28:19)?

2. Are the texts that say Jesus is equal to the Father in the majority? (See pp. 10-12.)

3. **Is it impossible** for Jesus to be both part of the Trinity, and yet not part?

4. Can we assume safely that God does not lie or teach two contradictory views in His word?

5. In most Bibles there is a note in the margin by Micah 5:2, which refers to the Messiah, as **from everlasting, from the days of eternity**. Could Jesus be a created being and be around from the days of eternity?

If we diagram our findings, it will look like this:

Jesus is fully divine, equal to the Father, part of the Trinity.

1. Gen. 1:26
2. Gen. 3:22
3. Gen. 11:7
4. Ex. 3:13-14
5. Neh. 9:6-15
6. Isa 6:8
7. Isaiah 9:6
8. Micah 5:2
9. Mt. 28:19
10. Jn. 1:1-3, 10, 14
11. Jn. 5:17, 18
12. Jn. 8:56-59
13. Jn. 10:30, 33
14. Jn. 14:28
15. Jn. 17:5
16. Acts 4:10-12
17. 1 Cor. 10:1-4
18. Eph. 3:9
19. Phil. 2:5-8
20. Col. 1:14-16
21. Heb. 1:2
22. James 4:12
23. Rev. 3:14

~~**Jesus is a created being; not divine and not equal to the Father.**~~

DEATH

Once you start searching through the Bible, subject by subject, and looking for the Big Picture, you will find that the two or three texts that seem to be out of line will become obvious. You will be able to pick them out very quickly and will see that they really are not contradictoary to the rest. With the Bible as the only guide, you will be able to distinguish truth from error.

Let me reemphasize that in every study, in nearly every subject, there are at least two or three verses that seem to contradict the Big Picture. Many times you will find that the majority of the texts on the subject make it very clear, but there are always a few tests that seem to muddy the water. Invariably, there is some cult or denomination that has built a whole doctrine on those few texts! Having taken a stand that is in opposition to the Big Picture, they must continually explain and twist the majority of the texts so that they support a doctrine that is built on two or three texts instead of the majority.

Let us move on and once again apply the ABC's of Bible study to another subject to get better acquainted with the method and our Bibles. This time let us look at the texts that deal with the subject of **death and what happens to a person who dies.** This is a controversial subject and there are two main views. Note carefully both views and the difference between them as listed below:

1. **Man has an immortal soul that never dies. When individuals die, they go directly to their reward, heaven or hell. These dead are in spirit form watching what happens on earth.**

2. **Man's soul is mortal or dies at death. When individuals die, they do not go anywhere, but are asleep in the grave, unconscious. Dead people do not know anything, go anywhere, or do anything, but are waiting for the second coming of Jesus, when they will be resurrected to life to receive their reward, either heaven or hell.**

Which view is correct? **If** view #1 is correct, then view #2 **must** be erroneous or vice versa! **Did God** allow His prophets to write two contradicting views, so as to confuse the sincere Christian who earnestly desires to know truth?

At this point we must ask ourselves, "Which view is based on the majority of the texts in the Bible, and which view is based on the four or five that seem to be out of line with the Big Picture on this subject?" If we line up the texts that each side quotes and then apply the ABC's of Bible study, we will find the Big Picture and again prove that God does not lie and contradict Himself in His Word. The four or five texts that are out of line with the majority will emerge, and **truth** will appear as God intended it, shining as a light in a dark place. The Psalmist describes God's Word as "a lamp unto my feet, and a light unto my path" (Psm. 119:105).

NOTE: If in my list of texts, you feel that I have left out an important text that has bearing on that subject, then you can add that text to your list and carefully search for **truth.** The purpose of this book is not to teach the doctrine of one church over another, but to teach a method of Bible study that will help to clarify some confusing subjects and draw the heart closer to Jesus, as He **is** "the way, the truth, and the life" (Jn. 14:6).

Let's line up the texts.

Dead people are sleeping unconsciously. The dead know nothing and are waiting in the grave for the second coming of Jesus to receive their reward. Man's soul is mortal and dies.

The dead go to their reward at death and man's soul never dies.

1. **Gen 2:17** God said to man, if you sin, **you will die.**
2. **Gen. 3:4** Satan tells the first lie: **you will not die.**
3. **Deut. 31:16, 27** Moses' **death is called sleep.**
4. **2 Sam. 7:12** David's death and burial, "...thou shalt **sleep** with thy fathers..."
5. **I Ki. 1:21** David's death and burial, "...the king shall **sleep** with his fathers..."
6. **1 Ki. 2:10** "So David **slept** with his fathers, **and was buried** in the city of David."
7. **1 Ki. 11:21** "And when Hadad heard in Egypt that David **slept** with his fathers..."

Dead people are sleeping unconsciously. The dead know nothing and are waiting in the grave for the second coming of Jesus to receive their reward. Man's soul is mortal and dies.

The dead go to their reward at death and man's soul never dies.

8. **1 Ki. 11:43** "And Solomon **slept** with his fathers, and was buried..."

9. **1 Ki. 14:31** "And Rehoboam **slept** with his fathers, **and was buried** with his fathers..."

10. **1 Ki. 15:8** "And Abijam **slept** with his fathers; and they **buried** him..."

11. **1 Ki. 15:24** "And Asa **slept** with his fathers, **and was buried** with his fathers..."

12. **1 Ki. 16:6** "So Baasha **slept** with his fathers, and was **buried**..."

13. **1 Ki. 16:28** "So Omri **slept** with his fathers, and was **buried**..."

14. **1 Ki. 22:40** "So Ahab **slept** with his fathers..."

15. **1 Ki. 22:50** "And Jehoshaphat **slept** with his fathers, and was **buried** with his fathers..."

Dead people are sleeping unconsciously. The dead know nothing and are waiting in the grave for the second coming of Jesus to receive their reward. Man's soul is mortal and dies.

The dead go to their reward at death and man's soul never dies.

16. **2 Ki. 8:24** "And Joram **slept** with his fathers, and was **buried** with his fathers..."

17. **2 Ki. 10:35** "And Jehu **slept** with his fathers: and they buried him..."

18. **2 Ki. 13:9** "And Jehoahaz **slept** with his fathers; and they buried him..."

19. **2 Ki. 13:13** "And Joash **slept** with his fathers...and Joash was buried..."

20. **2 Ki. 14:16** "And Jehoash **slept** with his fathers, and was buried..."

21. **2 Ki. 15:7** "So Azariah **slept** with his fathers; and they buried him with his fathers..."

22. **2 Ki. 15:22** "And Menahem **slept** with his fathers..."

23. **2 Ki. 15:38** "And Jotham **slept** with his fathers, and was buried..."

Dead people are sleeping unconsciously. The dead know nothing and are waiting in the grave for the second coming of Jesus to receive their reward. Man's soul is mortal and dies.

The dead go to their reward at death and man's soul never dies.

24. **2 Ki. 16:20** "And Ahaz **slept** with his fathers, and was buried..."

25. **2 Ki. 20:21** "And Hezekiah **slept** with his fathers..."

26. **2 Ki. 21:18** "And Manasseh **slept** with his fathers, and was buried..."

27. **2 Ki. 24:6** "So Jehoiakim **slept** with his fathers..."

28. **2 Chron. 26:23** "So Uzziah **slept** with his fathers, and they buried him with his fathers in the field..."

29. **Job 7:8-10, 21** Those that are dead, "**come up no *more*,**" but "**sleep in the dust**..."

30. **Job 21:23-30 The dead lie in the dust**, and the wicked are reserved to the day of destruction.

31. **Psm. 6:5** "For in death *there* is no remembrance of thee: in the grave who shall give thee thanks?

Dead people are sleeping unconsciously. The dead know nothing and are waiting in the grave for the second coming of Jesus to receive their reward. Man's soul is mortal and dies.

↑ (32.) **Psm. 13:3** "...lest I sleep **the *sleep of* death**."

↑ (33.) **Psm. 115:17** "The dead praise not the LORD, neither any that go down into silence."

↑ (34.) **Psm. 146:4** "His breath goeth forth, he returneth to his earth; in that very day his thoughts perish."

The dead go to their reward at death and man's soul never dies.

↑ (35.) **Eccl. 9:5-6, 10** "...the dead know not anything...for *there is* no work, nor device, nor knowledge, nor wisdom, in the grave..."

← (36.) **Eccl. 12:7** "Then shall the dust return to the earth as it was: and the spirit shall return unto God who gave it."

↑ (37.) **Eze. 18:4, 20** "...the **soul** that sinneth, **it shall die**."

Dead people are sleeping unconsciously. The dead know nothing and are waiting in the grave for the second coming of Jesus to receive their reward. Man's soul is mortal and dies.

↑ (38.) **Dan. 12:2** Speaking of the end of earth's history, when Jesus will come, Daniel says, "And many of them that **sleep in the dust** of the earth shall awake..."

↑ (39.) **Mt. 13:39-40** The harvest (or judgement) is at "the end of the world."

↑ (40.) **Mk. 5:35, 39** Referring to a dead girl, Jesus said, "the damsel is not dead, but sleepeth."

The dead go to their reward at death and man's soul never dies.

← (41.) **Lk. 16:19-31** The rich man and a beggar named Lazarus went to their reward at death.

← (42.) **Lk. 23:43** Jesus told a thief "... Verily I say unto thee, To day shalt thou be with me in paradise."

↑ (43.) **Jn. 5:28-29** "Marvel not at this: for the hour is coming, in the which all that are **in the graves** shall hear his voice..."

Dead people are sleeping unconsciously. The dead know nothing and are waiting in the grave for the second coming of Jesus to receive their reward. Man's soul is mortal and dies.

The dead go to their reward at death and man's soul never dies.

↑ (44.) **Jn. 11:11-14** Jesus calls death, "**sleep**."

↑ (45.) **Jn. 11:23-24** Martha said to Jesus, "I know that he (dead Lazarus) shall rise again in the resurrection **at the last day**."

↑ (46.) **Acts 2:29, 34** "...the patriarch David...is both dead and buried..." and "...**is not** ascended into the heavens..."

↑ (47.) **Acts 13:36** "For David...fell on sleep, and was laid unto his fathers, and saw corruption."

↑ (48.) **1 Cor. 15:6, 20** Paul calls death, **sleep.**

↑ (49.) **1 Cor. 15:51-55** Paul refers to the dead as **sleeping**.

← (50.) **2 Cor. 5:1-8** "...willing rather to be absent from the body, and to be present with the Lord."

Dead people are sleeping unconsciously. The dead know nothing and are waiting in the grave for the second coming of Jesus to receive their reward. Man's soul is mortal and dies.

51. **Phil. 1:23-24** Paul says, "For I am in a strait betwixt two, having a desire to depart and to be with Christ... Nevertheless to abide in the flesh is more needful for you."

52. **1 Thes. 4:13-17** Paul calls the dead believers, "those that **sleep**."

53. **1 Tim. 6:16** God "...only hath immortality..."

The dead go to their reward at death and man's soul never dies.

54. **2 Tim. 4:1, 8** "...the Lord Jesus Christ, who shall judge the quick and the dead **at his appearing**... there is laid up for me a crown of righteousness, which the Lord... shall give me **at that day:** and not to me only, but unto all them also that love his appearing."

55. **1 Pet. 3:19** "By which also he went and preached unto the spirits in prison."

Dead people are sleeping unconsciously. The dead know nothing and are waiting in the grave for the second coming of Jesus to receive their reward. Man's soul is mortal and dies.

56. **1 Pet. 4:6** "For this cause was the gospel preached also to them that are dead, that they might be judged according to men in the flesh, but live according to God in the spirit."

57. **2 Pet. 2:4, 9** God has reserved the wicked, and the fallen angels, until the day of judgment.

The dead go to their reward at death and man's soul never dies.

58. **Rev. 6:9-10** "...I saw under the alter the soul of them that were slain for the word of God,...and they cried with a loud voice, saying, How long, O Lord..."

59. **Rev. 20:4** "...and *I saw* the souls of them that were beheaded for the witness of Jesus...and they lived and reigned with Christ a thousand years."

60. **Rev. 22:12** Jesus brings his rewards with him, **when He comes** the second time.

As we line up the texts in the Big Picture, we can know with certainty which view the majority of texts support. At this point, some may say, if you want to support one view over the other, all you have to do is find more texts to support the view that you prefer, thus making it the Big Picture. That would be true, if in fact **you could find** a majority of texts to support any view, **but you can not**! The majority of texts supporting the Big Picture just seem to pile up, while the support for the erroneous view is always weak. The texts that support the false view are few in number and **more just cannot be found**!

The Bible seems to follow the rule that there are more texts on the one view than the other; thus the truth always emerges as the Big Picture. The one subject that comes closest to being the exception to the rule is the subject of hell, and we will cover that in another chapter.

Let me restate the above as it is crucial to sincere Bible study. No matter how hard one digs to find texts that are related on one subject, a majority will emerge, and by the sheer weight of the texts available, you will find **truth**. This may be difficult for some to accept. They may begin to realize that they are backing a false view, and will not want to give it up in light of truth. For the sincere Christian this one rule of Bible study (the "B" of the ABC's) will be like a breath of fresh air in a stuffy room that is already overcrowded.

The Big Picture principle will help in another way, too. As you establishe one or two of the basic doctrines of the Bible, you will begin to build one doctrine on another and will see the relationship of one doctrine to another. It has a snowball effect, so that you can build your beliefs on a broader and broader basis of truth.

It is a method of Bible study that I am introducing and not one doctrine over another. Remember, God does not lie and contradict Himself in His Word; so ultimately one view **must** be truth and the other error. When we find the majority of verses in our study, indicating one particular belief, then we will check our findings by examining the context ("C" of the ABC's) of the minority, to see if, in fact, they do fit into the Big Picture without being twisted. Let us examine the findings of our study on death.

The dead go to their reward at death and man's soul never dies.	**Dead people are sleeping unconsciously. The dead know nothing and are waiting in the grave for the second coming of Jesus to receive their reward. Man's soul is mortal and dies.**		
#36	#1	#18	#35
#41	#2	#19	#37
#42	#3	#20	#38
#50	#4	#21	#39
#51	#5	#22	#40
#55	#6	#23	#43
#56	#7	#24	#44
#58	#8	#25	#45
#59	#9	#26	#46
	#10	#27	#47
Total support = 9 texts	#11	#28	#48
	#12	#29	#49
	#13	#30	#52
	#14	#31	#53
	#15	#32	#54
	#16	#33	#57
	#17	#34	#60
	Total Support = 51 texts		

The majority of the texts **clearly** support the view that **the dead are sleeping**, waiting for Jesus to come the second time and give them their reward.

In order to be extra careful about this subject, since it is a very controversial issue, we will draw our minority and majority conclusions in three different ways. Our first chart is above, with all the texts in our list. If all of the texts about people in the Old Testament "sleeping with their fathers (or dying) and being buried," were combined into one reference then texts #3 through #28 would be counted as one in our list, and we would draw our conclusions about the minority and majority with the chart below.

The dead go to their reward at death and man's soul never dies.	**Dead people are sleeping unconsciously. The dead know nothing and are waiting in the grave for the second coming of Jesus to receive their reward. Man's soul is mortal and dies.**		
#36	#1	#35	#47
#41	#2	#37	#48
#42	#3-28 = 1 ref.)	#38	#49
#50	#29	#39	#52
#51	#30	#40	#53
#55	#31	#43	#54
#56	#32	#44	#57
#58	#33	#45	#60
#59	#34	#46	
Total Support = 9 texts	*Total Support = 26 texts*		

Even after discounting the many texts about people "sleeping with their fathers (dying) and being buried," the majority and minority are still easily distinguishable.

If we go even a step further and throw out all the Old Testament references and just compare the New Testament references, then our chart would look like this:

The dead go to their reward at death and man's soul never dies.	**Dead people are sleeping unconsciously. The dead know nothing and are waiting in the grave for the second coming of Jesus to receive their reward. Man's soul is mortal and dies.**	
#41	#39	#48
#42	#40	#49
#50	#43	#52
#51	#44	#53
#55	#45	#54
#56	#46	#57
#58	#47	#60
#59		
Total Support = 8 texts	*Total Support = 14 texts*	

Even if we did just accept **part** of the Scriptures (the New Testament), **we would still find the majority and the minority have not changed places**. Of course we cannot selectively choose which part of the Scriptures we would like to believe, but we must accept **all** of God's Word.

The majority of the texts clearly support the view that the dead are sleeping, waiting for Jesus to come the second time and give them their reward.

Now notice the list that **appears** to be in contradiction with the Big Picture, saying that the dead go directly to their reward at death (from our original chart on p. 33). If we apply the "C" of the ABC's (Context) to the list that is unquestionably in the minority, we will see if, in fact, these texts are **out of line** with the Big Picture or if they just **appear to be** at first glance.

Text #36 **Eccl. 12:7** "Then shall the dust return to the earth as it was: and the spirit shall return unto God who gave it."

The text gives us a detailed account of what happens to **all people** at death. The questionable part of the verse is "and the spirit goes back to God...." What is it that goes back to God at death? It is the "spirit!" The Hebrew word "ruach," which is translated "spirit," has many different meanings in the Old Testament. Listed below are a few examples of how the word is translated:

wind...117 times
spirit of God ....94 times
spirit ....76 times
breath..33 times
living principle in men and animals.25 times
moral character.................................16 times
mind ....9 times
seat of emotions ....3 times

So far as man is concerned, in the 379 instances of the use of this word in the Old Testament, it **never** denotes an intelligent entity apart from a physical body.

To understand what goes back to God at death, let us look at how man was put together by God in the beginning.

Gen. 2:7 "And the LORD God formed man *of* the **dust** of the ground and breathed into his nostrils the **breath of life;** and man **became a living soul.**"

body = dust of the ground
spirit = the breath of life

BODY + SPIRIT = SOUL

In both Job 27:3 and 33:4 the terms "spirit" and "the breath of life" are used interchangeably.

Notice that it is the combination of the body plus the spirit that **equals** the soul. Man was **not** given a soul but when the spirit (or breath of life) was put together with the body, **man became** a living soul (or being).

Now if we apply this to our text of Eccl. 12:7 to gain insight, we find harmony in this text and the Big Picture. When a person dies, whether he is good or bad, the dust (body) returns unto the earth. (We bury the dead in the ground.) The spirit, spark of life, or breath of life that originally came from God at birth to give life, returns to God who gave it. This is not a disembodied spirit that floats around in heaven or hell because the dead do not know anything, and they do not praise the Lord. (Review texts #33 and #35.) This text simply indicates that the breath of life (or the spirit) returns to the source of all life, God. The person is dead and knows nothing. As it states in James 2:26, "...the body without the spirit is dead..."

Man is no longer a living soul (or a living being as the RSV translates Gen. 2:7). The two components that made up the living soul are separated, and the soul, or being, or person, sleeps unconsciously until Jesus comes the second time as the Lifegiver on resurrection morning (Isa. 26:19, Jn. 5:28-29; Jn. 11:11-14, 23-26).

Text #41 Luke 16:19-31 The rich man and Lazarus

Many consider this story and its implications on the Biblical teachings of "death," "hell," and "when a person receives his reward." If we consider the story to be a literal teaching, rather than a parable that Jesus used to illustrate a point, then we would be saying:

1. The dead receive their reward (heaven or hell) immediately at death.

2. Dead people still know what is going on among the living.

According to the Big Picture, the two above statements could **not possibly be true**, or it would mean that God is contradicting Himself and lying, and that cannot happen.

We need to look carefully at this text to find the true meaning. This **is** a parable that Jesus used to illustrate two main points. Every detail of the parable **is not to be applied literally.** The context around this verse will support our conclusions; so let us examine the text.

1. Jesus' two conclusions:

   a. There is a fixed gulf (or chasm) between the living and the dead, so that the dead cannot pass back and forth to life (vs. 26).

b. If living people will not listen to the Bible and what it teaches, then they would not listen, even **if** someone did come back from the dead and try to persuade them to change their views (vs. 31).

2. The starting phrase (Lk. 16:19) of the rich man and Lazarus is **the same as many other parables** that Jesus told in the Gospel of Luke. Note the following comparative list:

a. There was **a certain creditor**...	Lk. 7:41
b. **A certain man**...	Lk. 10:30
c. The ground of **a certain rich man**...	Lk. 12:16
d. **A certain man**...	Lk. 13:6
e. **A certain man**...	Lk. 14:16
f. **A certain man**...	Lk. 15:11
g. There was **a certain rich man**...	Lk.16:1
* h. There was **a certain rich man**...	Lk. 16:19
i. **A certain nobleman**...	Lk. 19:12

* verse in question

3. The story of "the rich man" is listed in most commentaries, concordances, and backs of Bibles, in the same list with all the other parables.

4. **If** the rich man and Lazarus were to be taken literally then the following would have to be true:

   a. Verse 22: Abraham's bosom would be heaven. (According to Heb. 11:8-10, **it is not,** because Abraham searched for heaven while living in tents.)

b. Verses 23-24: People in hell have parts of their bodies. (According to Mt. 10:28, the body is destroyed in the fires of hell.)

c. Verses 22-24: Dead people know what is going on around them. (According to Eccl. 9:5-6, 10; Psm. 6:5; 115:17; and 146:4, that cannot be true.)

d. Verse 22-24: People go straight to their reward **at death**. (According to Acts 2:29, 34; Jn. 5:28-29; 2 Tim. 4:1, 8 and Rev 22:12, people **do not** receive their reward **at death**, but at the second coming of Jesus.)

Our conclusion, in light of the context and the Big Picture, **must be** that **this is a parable** Jesus told to illustrate His two main points as outlined under #1 above. Jesus Himself was a good example of the points that He was trying to make. Even though Moses and the prophets told of His true role as the suffering sacrifice, many would not listen to Him and believe that He was the Messiah. They refused to believe Him even though He would rise from the dead.

Therefore, we can conclude that this text, if understood correctly in light of its context, points in the same direction as the rest of the verses on this subject. It fits into the true picture of what happens to a person when he dies.

Text #42 **Luke 23:43** "...Verily I say unto thee, To day shalt thou be with me in paradise."

This verse, at first reading, appears to say that both Jesus and the thief went to paradise that day. If there is one verse that is quoted more often than any other to go straight to heaven, it is this one. **Is there a way** to harmonize this text so that it lends its support to the Big Picture? Can it be done without twisting the meaning of the text? **Yes**, there is a way to understand this text that is in accordance with other verses on this subject.

In order for there to be harmony in the Bible surrounding this text, we must be able to reconcile the following three items that I have listed below for clarification purposes.

1. Jesus words to the thief on Friday (Lk. 23:43)

2. Jesus words to Mary on Sunday (Jn. 20:17)

3. The Big Picture

On the resurrection morning (Jn. 20:17), Jesus told Mary that He **had not** been to see His Father yet. There are many verses in the Bible that tell us Heaven and Paradise are one and the same place. In 2 Cor. 12:2, 4 Paul uses the terms "third heaven" and "paradise" interchangeably. Rev. 2:7 tells us the tree of life is "in the midst of the paradise of God." In Rev. 22:1-2 the tree of life is also mentioned to be in heaven near the throne of God.

If we understand Jesus to be saying to the thief that He and the thief would be going to Paradise that day (Friday), then Jesus' words in Lk. 23:43 would be in contradiction with the Big Picture and Jesus' own words to Mary when He told her on Sunday morning that He had not yet been to see His Father. Let us carefully reexamine our text that seems to be out of line with the Big Picture.

Luke 23:43 "...Verily I say unto thee, To day shalt thou be with me in paradise."

There is an answer that does justice to the text, to Jesus' statement to Mary (Jn. 20:17), and to the Big Picture. Read the following illustration carefully:

↓
Woman, without her, man is a beast.

Who is the beast in the above statement? **Man**, of course! But notice how drastically the meaning of a sentence can be altered if we change, not the words, but just a comma.

↓
Woman, without her man, is a beast.

Now who is the beast? **Woman**, of course! Compare the two statements carefully and note that the only change is in the placing of a comma. What a difference it makes in the meaning of the sentence! So it is in our TEXT #42. Note the difference below.

"Verily I say unto thee,
To day shalt thou be with me in paradise."

"Verily I say unto thee To day,
shalt thou be with me in paradise."

Note, in the first illustration, the verse is saying that the thief and Jesus were going directly to paradise that day.

In the second illustration of the verse, Jesus is promising the thief that He will be in Paradise with him.

In other words, Jesus was saying, "I am telling you today, while we both are hanging here on the cross, with no hope of earthly help, you will be with Me in Paradise." The thief **did** ask Jesus (vs. 42) to remember him, not that day, but **when He came into His kingdom.**

Someone might say, at this point, if you change a comma from one place to another, wouldn't you be changing the Bible, or twisting it? If you do a little research, by asking any Bible scholar (teacher or professor) of **any** denomination, you will discover that the commas, the periods, and all the punctuation, even the verse divisions are not in the original scrolls that the prophets wrote. They were added later by well meaning people who wanted to make the Bible easier to understand.

In fact, the New Testament Greek was written in capital letters with no divisions between the words. The phrase (Rev. 1:11) when transliterated into English capital letters would look like this:

"IAMALPHAANDOMEGA" (English)

"EGOEIMITOALPHAKAITOO" (Greek)

Since ancient manuscripts had no punctuation marks or verse divisions when they were written, there could very easily be a misplaced comma. Dividing the Bible into chapters was introduced in the 13th century and verse divisions came around three centuries after that. Therefore, we can safely conclude that God did not inspire the commas, as there were none in the original parchments and manuscripts.

By changing the comma in Lk. 23:43, we bring this verse into line with the Big Picture. We preserve the integrity of Jesus (Jn. 20:17 and Lk. 23:43) and prove our original assumption to be correct that God does not lie and contradict himself.

For those who may still have doubts about commas being misplaced in the Scriptures, notice that **there is another comma misplaced**. It is a little more obvious and is found in the King James Version of the Bible. The verse is Acts 19:12.

> "So that from his body were brought unto the sick handkerchiefs or aprons, and the diseases departed from them..."

This verse says that God performed special miracles through Paul, even allowing him to heal people by touching them with his handkerchief. Notice **if the statement is read as it is punctuated**, with the comma misplaced (only in the KJV), then it says that the handkerchiefs were sick. This is an obvious mistake that was corrected in all of the newer translations but illustrates that the commas in the Bible were not inspired by God. Centuries after the scrolls were written, men who punctuated them misplaced a comma that has caused many woes to the ardent student of the Word trying to find the harmonious Big Picture.

TEXT #50 **2 Cor. 5:1-8** "...willing rather to be absent from the body, and to be present with the Lord.

From a superficial reading of 2 Cor. 5:1-8, (particularly vs. 6-8), some have concluded that the soul of the Christian goes immediately at death to be "present with the Lord," and that Paul desired to be with the Lord so much (vs. 2) that he desired death. But in vs. 3 and 4, Paul describes death as a state of being naked or unclothed. Paul hoped to avoid this state of death and looked forward (as all earnest Christians do) to the time when he would be changed and put on immortality. (See 1 Cor. 15:51-55; 1 Thess. 4:15-17; and 2 Tim. 4:1, 8.)

Careful scrutiny of all of Paul's statements on death show that **Paul did not believe in a state between death and the resurrection**, in which men go to be present with the Lord as "naked" or "disembodied" spirits. Compare

Rom. 8:22-23 where Paul states that we want to have our immortal bodies, **but we wait for them**.

TEXT #51 **Phil. 1:23-24** Paul says, "For I am in a strait betwixt two, having a desire to depart, and to be with Christ... Nevertheless to abide in the flesh is more needful for you."

It is quite obvious in these verses that Paul wishes for the return of the Saviour. When Paul compares staying on this earth or being in heaven with the literal presence of Jesus, he chooses heaven and Jesus without batting an eye. This verse (24), by itself, might be misconstrued to say that Paul does not think he will be "in the flesh" if he departs. His words in vs. 24 "Nevertheless to abide in the flesh is more needful for you," are worthy of careful consideration. If this and 2 Cor. 5:1-8 were the only verses that Paul wrote on this subject, then I, too, might think that Paul planned on going straight to heaven, in spirit form, at death. Notice all of Paul's statements on this subject. In TEXTS #48, 49, 52, 53, and 54, Paul makes it very clear that **he believes that the dead are sleeping.**

TEXT #54 makes it abundantly clear that Paul expects to receive his crown, **at that day** (the second coming of Jesus). It is clear that Paul does not mention any time lapse between the "departing to be with Christ" and the "remaining in the flesh" in this text. But he does give those details in his other comments on death. Also, if death is like sleep, as Paul calls it so often, then the dead will not be aware of the time that passes after they die while they are in the ground sleeping. As far as the dead person knows, one minute or a hundred years will be the same, since they are oblivious to all passing of time. The next thing that will affect them will be Christ calling them forth to life eternal **at His appearing**.

I am glad that we have so many statements about death from Paul and the other Bible writers. We can correctly understand the difficult verses of the Bible, and not build a doctrine on a few verses that appear contradictory to the majority.

TEXT #55 **1 Pet. 3:19** "By which also he went and preached unto the spirits in prison."

TEXT #56 **1 Pet. 4:6** "For this cause was the gospel preached also to them that are dead, that they might be judged according to men in the flesh, but live according to God in the spirit."

These references are the ones that the doctrine of purgatory is built upon. Since these texts are so closely related and cover the same idea, I will deal with them together.

Many have received the idea from these texts that there are people in a spirit world or prison that is between life, death, and heaven. At the spirit prison, they (the dead) have the gospel preached to them. This would contradict the clear statements of Jesus and other Bible writers who say that death is like sleep, and a person feels nothing, thinks nothing, knows nothing, while he is dead. Notice a few things about our first text (#55, 1 Pet. 3:19).

1. The first two words, "By which"

2. The last four words, "the spirits in prison"

These two phrases are crucial to our understanding of this text. Both phrases can be interpreted in two very different ways. Notice the chart below that explains the two different ways of interpretation.

Purgatory Belief	**Dead Sleeping**
1. "By which" refers to Christ (vs. 18) who went to preach to dead people of Noah's day.	1. "By which" refers to the Holy Spirit (vs. 18) that worked through Noah (vs. 20) to warn people for God.
2. "The spirits in prison" refers to a spirit world where disembodied spirits go and are held in prison.	2. "The spirits in prison" refers to living people that are in prison to **sin**. Jesus came to earth to set the captives of **sin** free, and openly stated this in Lk. 4:18 when He quoted Isa. 61:1.

Read the whole verse of Isa. 61:1. Then read the story around Lk. 4:18 and how Christ applied it to His ministry.

> "The Spirit of the Lord GOD *is* upon me; because the LORD hath anointed me to preach the good tidings unto the meek; he hath sent me to bind up the brokenhearted, to proclaim liberty to the **captives**, and the opening of the **prison** to *them that are* bound;"

The New American Bible (Catholic) has listed, in the margin next to 1 Pet. 3:19, the following comment:

> "There are various interpretations of this verse. It probably refers to the risen Christ making

> known to imprisoned souls His victory over sin and death" (NAB, p. 1356, paperback ed., Col. 2, last note).

From the three items listed above (comparison chart, Isa. 61:1 quote, and the Catholic note), **it is evident that this verse is controversial and difficult to understand**. Note from the following that our second text, #56 is also difficult and controversial.

Our second text (#56, 1 Pet. 4:6) can also be interpreted to be saying two very opposite things, as the note in the NAB (Catholic) translations states so clearly.

> "4:6; The gospel was preached even to the dead; this may refer to bringing the benefits of salvation to the 'spirits' in prison (cf 3:19), or to the preaching of the gospel to Christians who have since died" (NAB, p. 1357, paperback ed., Col. 1, first note).

Many Bible scholars have wrestled with these difficult verses, trying to understand them correctly. Note how the NIV (New International Version) translates 1 Pet. 4:6.

> "For this is the reason the gospel was preached, even to those **who are now dead**, so that they might be judged according to men in regard to the body, but live according to God in regard to the spirit."

I am glad for the Big Picture and the clarity that it brings to the interpretation of verses such as these (TEXTS #55 and 56). **They are difficult and clearly have two possible ways of being understood**. If 1 Pet. 3:19 and 4:6 were the only texts that we had on the subject of death, their interpretation might be open to question. Since they are not our only light, and we have the Big Picture to help guide us, we can know for sure how to "rightly divide the Word of truth."

1 Pet. 3:19 **states** that Christ (salvation) was preached to the people of Noah's time, by the Holy Spirit, through the ministry of Noah.

1 Pet. 4:6 **tells us** that the gospel was preached to Christians while they were alive, but they are now dead. It is **not** saying that Jesus went to some mystical "spirit world" to preach the gospel to the disembodied spirits that were there. (I have also heard people use Eph. 4:9 to present this same misinterpretation, but if you check any modern translation, it says Christ descended to the earth, and not "the lower parts of the earth.")

TEXT #58 **Rev. 6:9-10** "...I saw under the alter the soul of them that were slain for the word of God...and they cried with a loud voice, saying, How long, O Lord..."

Text #59 **Rev. 20:4** "...and *I saw* the souls of them that were beheaded for the witness of Jesus...and they lived and reigned with Christ a thousand years."

Since these texts are also similar, I will deal with them together. In both of these texts "souls" are mentioned that have endured persecution for the Word of God. Everything in prophecy cannot be taken literally. Some things are symbolic. If we were to interpret these texts literally to build a case for disembodied spirits, we would not only be twisting prophetic interpretation, but we would also make John contradict himself (TEXT #43, 44, 45 and 60).

According to what we have already studied, the soul is made up of two parts, the body and the spirit, and unless the two parts are together, **there is no** living being or soul. The interpretation of the verses must therefore be symbolic, showing in symbolism that whenever God's people are in distress or persecuted, they yearn or cry out to Him for help. If this verse were to be taken literally, then perhaps we should take Gen. 4:10 literally when it says the blood of Abel cried out to God when he was slain. In this instance, as well as in our verses (#58 and 59), it is saying that God's people do cry out to Him, and He is aware of their needs and cries.

Ardent students of the Word may be able to find two or three more texts that "appear" to back the idea of going straight to heaven at death. That changes things a little, **very little.** Instead of there being 51 texts for soul sleep and 9 opposed, the results might be (in another study) 51 for soul sleep and 12 opposed. We should still assume that God does not lie in His Word and contradict Himself.

Our final diagram looks like this:

Dead people are sleeping unconsciously. The dead know nothing and are waiting in the grave for the second coming of Jesus to receive their reward. Man's soul is mortal and dies.

The dead go to their reward at death and man's soul never dies.

1. Gen. 2:17
2. Gen. 3:4
3. Deut. 31:16, 27
4. 2 Sam. 7:12
5. 1 Ki. 1:21
6. 1 Ki. 2:10
7. 1 Ki. 11:21
8. 1 Ki. 11:43
9. 1 Ki. 14:31
10. 1 Ki. 15:8
11. 1 Ki. 15:24
12. 1 Ki. 16:6
13. 1Ki. 16:28
14. 1 Ki. 22:40
15. 1 Ki. 22:50
16. 2 Ki. 8:24
17. 2 Ki. 10:35
18. 2 Ki. 13:9
19. 2 Ki. 13:13
20. 2 Ki. 14:16
21. 2 Ki. 15:7
22. 2 Ki. 15:22
23. 2 Ki. 15:38
24. 2 Ki. 16:20
25. 2 Ki. 20:21
26. 2 Ki. 21:18
27. 2 Ki. 24:6
28. 2 Chrn. 26:23
29. Job 7:8-10, 21
30. Job 21:23-30
31. Psm. 6:5
32. Psm. 13:3
33. Psm. 115:17
34. Psm. 146:4
35. Eccl. 9:5-6, 10
36. Eccl. 12:7
37. Eze. 18:4, 20
38. Dan. 12:2
39. Mt. 13:39-40
40. Mk. 5:35, 39
41. Lk. 16:19-31
42. Lk. 23:43
43. Jn. 5:28-29
44. Jn. 11:11-14
45. Jn. 11:23-24
46. Acts 2:29, 34
47. Acts 13:36
48. 1 Cor. 15:6, 20
49. 1 Cor. 15:51-55
50. 2 Cor. 5:1-8
51. Phil. 1:23-24
52. 1 Thess. 4:13-17
53. 1 Tim. 6:16
54. 2 Tim. 4:1, 8
55. 1 Pet. 3:19
56. 1 Pet. 4:6
57. 2 Pet. 2:4, 9
58. Rev. 6:9-10
59. Rev. 20:4
60. Rev. 22:12

Some who have never studied the subject of death by the ABC method might claim that the dead go straight to their reward. There are more problems Scripturally with that view than solutions. For example,

1. If a person did go straight to heaven at death, and was in eternal happiness and not just asleep, then we could assume they would be happy praising the Lord for taking them to heaven. Right? No! Wrong! The Bible states clearly, "The dead praise not the LORD, neither any that go down **into silence**" (TEXT #33).

2. If the dead go straight to Heaven at death, how could Jesus bring His rewards with Him when He comes, as indicated in TEXTS #39, 54, and 60? Those dead who have supposedly gone to heaven would have to return when Jesus comes, get into their graves where He said they would be, (TEXTS #43 and 52) and then be resurrected to receive the reward of everlasting life that they have already been enjoying. Does that sound logical?

3. If our departed loved ones were aware of our activities after death, how happy and peaceful would they be? If they watched us get hurt, struggle with a heavy financial burden, or remarry and love someone else, would that make them happy and able to enjoy eternal bliss? That does not sound like eternal bliss to me; **it sounds more like torture.**

4. Jer. 31:15-17 is a Messianic prophecy that predicted the death and slaughter of innocent children. It gives hope and reassurance to parents who have

> lost little children to death. It gives hope to grieving parents that they will see their little ones again and their "work will be rewarded." **If** the dead went straight to their reward **at death,** then in Jer. 31:15-17 it would say that the babies slain by Herod (Mt. 2:16-18) would come back from heaven where they were with Jesus. **It does not say that**! It says clearly that they will come back **from the land of the enemy**. Death is never a friend, but always an enemy. It separates us from our loved ones.

How good and right is the picture of death the Bible gives us when it says that the dead are "asleep" and "know nothing" of our activities and the goings on of this world. They are finally at true rest, with no more worries or cares, beyond the reach of pain, anguish and turmoil, awaiting the call of the Lifegiver, the One who said, "...I am the resurrection, and the life: he that believeth in me, though he were dead, yet shall he live..." (Jn. 11:25). What a day of rejoicing that will be! Families who have been long separated by the barrier of death will again be reunited. Then truly "Death is swallowed up in victory," and those people will say, "O death, where is thy sting? O grave, where *is* thy victory" (1 Cor. 15:55)?

Some may say, "I have proof that the dead do come back from the grave to communicate because my spouse or uncle (or someone else) did. I know about it, and it was real." They may even say that there is a story in the Bible that proves this type of thing happens and quote the story of Samuel. If you look this up in 1 Sam. 28, you will find the story, but note the following:

1. Verse 6 says that **it was not the Lord** who answered the request of Saul.

2. Saul said **God did not answer** his request by His prophets (vs. 15).

3. Samuel was a prophet of God.

4. Saul **thought** it was Samuel (vs. 14, 15).

If Saul **was not** answered by a prophet of God (and Samuel was God's prophet), **then who** answered the request of Saul when he worked through the spirit medium at Endor? One possible answer is that it was Satan and the powers of darkness, who will do anything to deceive "the very elect." Consider the following Scriptures.

1. **Mt. 24:24** "...show great signs and wonders...shall deceive the very elect."

2. **2 Cor. 11:13-14** "For such *are* false apostles... **transforming themselves** into the apostles of Christ."

3. **Rev. 16:14** "For **they are the spirits of devils**, working miracles..."

The Bible is very clear and **is opposed to all types of witchcraft and spirit mediums**. (See Deut. 18:10-12.) If you are still unsure about this subject, then take a moment to look up the following words in a concordance: divination, medium, soothsayers, witchcraft, etc. Make a new study from the findings.

I have purposely picked subjects from the Bible that are problematic, because I believe that they will illustrate the ABC concept of comparing Scripture with Scripture to arrive at truth, even in the face of great controversy.

The fact that a certain belief or bias is popular does not mean that it is true. **Popularity does not dictate truth!** If it did, then the popular concept in Jesus' time that He would be a Saviour from the Roman yoke of bondage and not a Savior from sin would have been true. **It wasn't!** Jesus was then and still is a Saviour from sin. The Jews had another concept of the coming Messiah, something other than a humble lamb, but that **did not** make their concept true.

If popularity of an idea makes something true, then the majority of the people must have been right when they cried, "Crucify Him, crucify Him." They were in the majority that morning at Jesus' trial. If, on the other hand, the Bible is what we use as our guide, and the Holy Spirit is promised to us to guide us into truth (Jn. 16:13), then, by comparing Scripture with Scripture, we will arrive at truth **whether or not** it is the popular view.

Then comes the hardest part of all, the decision. What means more to us, to be on the side of truth with perhaps the minority of believers, or to be with the popular view and the majority? If you have any doubts of where Jesus will be, then let me assure you that **He will always be standing by His Word**, whether or not it is the accepted or popular concept.

Heaven

One of the most unfortunate consequences of misunderstanding the Scriptures is making the desirable things of the Bible seem undesirable. When we teach or follow one doctrine of error, that one teaching does not stand alone as if it were an isolated island. It fills other doctrines with erroneous overtones. Such is the case with the popular teaching of death, and the overtones that it has on the subject of heaven.

The popular teaching of death, as we discussed in the last chapter, would have the dead person going to heaven in spirit form to watch what happens on earth. This misunderstanding of death has led people to believe that, when a person goes to heaven, all there is to do is sit around on a fluffy white cloud and play a harp. Some would refer to this type of existence as being eternal bliss; but if they were asked to just sit around now plucking a harp, they would soon refer to it as boring torment.

The Bible does mention that the redeemed play harps (Rev. 15:2), but **is that the extent of our activities** according to the Bible? Will we be spirit bodies with no substance, or real bodies that have substance?

There are three different places that are called "heaven" in the Bible and they are listed below:

1. **The first heaven**: where the birds fly and where the clouds form and bring rain to the earth (Gen. 1:20; 7:11; Deut. 11:11; Dan. 8:8; Rev. 19:17)

2. **The second heaven:** where the sun and stars are and the planets have their orbit (Gen. 1:14, 16-17; Isa. 13:10; Joel 2:30; Mt. 24:29)

3.The third heaven: where the throne of God is (I Ki. 8:30, 39; Psm. 11:4; 53:2; 80:14; 102:19; 139:8; 2 Cor. 12:2-4; Rev. 21 and 22).

In our study, we will focus upon the third heaven that Paul calls Paradise (2 Cor. 12:2-4). This is the place most Christians refer to when they speak of "heaven."

The Old and New Testament alike tell of a time and place when there will be "a new heaven and a new earth" that God creates (Isa. 65:17; Rev. 21:1). Many things will be different there. First, we will line up the texts that deal with some of the changes that will be in this "new heaven and new earth." Secondly, we will look at what the Bible says about the type of bodies that we will have when we get there.

Heaven is real, with things to do in the New Heaven and Earth

Nothing to do but float and play a harp

1. **Psm. 16:11** We will never get bored.
2. **Isa. 11:6-9** The animals will be tame.
3. **Isa. 33:24** There will be no sickness.
4. **Isa. 35:1-2** The desert will blossom like a rose.
5. **Isa. 35:5-6** There will be no deformities of any kind.

Heaven is real, with things to do in the New Heaven and Earth

↑

6. **Isa. 35:10** We will sing and play music.

↑

7. **Isa. 40:31** We will never get tired.

↑

8. **Isa. 60:18** There will be no more violence of any kind.

↑

9. **Isa. 65: 21-22** We will be able to build houses and plant gardens.

↑

Nothing to do but float and play a harp

10. **Isa. 65:24** Before we can even ask, God will answer us.

↑

11. **Isa. 65:25** Animals' diets will be changed.

↑

12. **Jer. 31:15-17** Babies who were slain, or have died will live again.

↑

13. **Zech. 8:5** There will be children playing there.

↑

14. **Mal. 4:2** We will grow up to our full stature and capabilities.

↑

15. **Mt. 8:11** We visit with the patriarchs and the prophets.

Heaven is real, with things to do in the New Heaven and Earth

↑

(16.) **Heb. 11:9-10, 16** There is a city there and God is the builder.

↑

(17.) **1 Jn. 3:2** We will be with Jesus and see Him face to face.

↑

(18.) **Rev. 2:7** The Tree of Life is in the midst of the city.

← (19.) **Rev. 15:2-3** The redeemed sing a new song and play harps.

Nothing to do but float and play a harp

↑

(20.) **Rev. 21:2** The city's name is the New Jerusalem.

↑

(21.) **Rev. 21:3** God will dwell with us.

↑

(22.) **Rev. 21:4** No tears, death or sorrow of any kind will be there.

↑

(23.) **Rev. 21:13-21** The city has walls made of jasper, and gates of pearls.

↑

(24.) **Rev. 21:21** The streets are like pure gold and yet clear like glass.

↑

(25.) **Rev. 21:23** There is no need of the sun, for Jesus is the light.

Heaven is real, with things to do in the New Heaven and Earth

↑

(26.) **Rev. 21:25** There will be no night there.

↑

Nothing to do but float and play a harp

(27.) **Rev. 22:1** The River of Life flows from the city.

↑

(28.) **Rev. 22:2** The leaves from the Tree of Life are for the healing of the nations.

Many have assumed that heaven is unreal and boring because of their concept of death and going straight to heaven in spirit form. From our study on death in the last chapter, we learned that no one goes straight to heaven in spirit form and just floats around. People who have died are sleeping in the grave, waiting for the call of the Lifegiver. We can see from our previous study that **when** Jesus resurrects those who are sleeping in the dust of the ground, they will have plenty to do in that new heaven and earth. But what will we be like? The Scriptures tell us plainly that we will be like Jesus after He was resurrected. Note the references below:

1. **Phil. 3:20-21** "...the LORD Jesus Christ: Who shall change our vile body, that it may be fashioned like unto his glorious body..."

2. **1 Jn. 3:2** "Beloved, now are we the sons of God, and it doth not yet appear what we shall be: but

we know that, when he shall appear, we shall be like him; for we shall see him as he is."

All we have to do is ask ourselves, what was Jesus' glorious body like? Does the Bible tell us? **Yes it does**! Let us line up the texts and see.

A changed, physical body like Jesus' glorious body

↑

1. **Lk. 24:36-43** "And as they thus spake, Jesus himself stood in the midst of them, and sayeth unto them, Peace *be* unto you. But they were terrified and affrighted, and supposed that they had seen **a spirit**. And he said unto them, Why are ye troubled? and why do thoughts arise in your hearts? Behold my hands and my feet, that it is I myself: **handle me**, and see; for a spirit hath not flesh and bones, **as ye see me have**. And when he had thus spoken, he shewed them *his* hands and *his* feet. And while they yet believed not for joy, and wondered, he said unto them, Have ye here any meat? And they gave him a piece of broiled fish, and of an honeycomb. And he took *it*, and did eat before them."

A spirit body only

A changed, physical body like Jesus' glorious body

↑

(2.) **Jn. 20:11-16** Jesus spoke to Mary in the garden, near the tomb, and was recognized by His voice and His appearance.

↑

(3.) **Jn. 20:26-29** Jesus stood among the disciples the second time and said to Thomas, "Reach hither thy finger, and behold my hands; and reach hither thy hand, and thrust *it* into my side: and be not faithless but believing..."

A spirit body only

↑

(4.) **1 Cor 13:12** "For now we see through a glass, darkly; but then face to face: now I know in part; but **then shall I know even as also I am known**."

← (5.) **1 Cor. 15:44** "It is sown a natural body; it is raised a spiritual body. There is a natural body, and there is a spiritual body."

← (6.) **1 Cor. 15:50** "Now this I say, brethren, that flesh and blood cannot inherit the kingdom of God; neither doth corruption inherit incorruption."

A changed, physical body like Jesus' glorious body

↑

(7.) **Phil. 3:20-21** "...the LORD Jesus Christ: **Who shall change** our vile body, that it may be fashioned **like unto his glorious body,** according to the working whereby he is able even to subdue all things unto himself."

A spirit body only

↑

(8.) **1 Jn. 3:2** "Beloved, now are we the sons of God, and it doth not yet appear what we shall be: but we know that, when he shall appear, **we shall be like him**; for we shall see him as he is."

The majority of the texts on this subject agree with the idea that we will have a changed, incorruptible, physical body. Let us look closely at the two texts that appear to be out of line.

TEXT #5 **1 Cor. 15:44** "It is sown a natural body; it is raised a spiritual body. There is a natural body, and there is a spiritual body."

Paul is here contrasting the existence of man in a physical body, that knows pain and death, with the body that we will have when we are given our spiritual bodies that know no pain. Paul is not saying that man is raised in the resurrection in a spirit form, without a physical body. That would contradict not only his own statement in Phil. 3:20, but the statements of John and Jesus in Lk. 24:36-43 and 1 Jn. 3:2. Our bodies will be changed, so that they are different, with no decay. They will still be patterned after the example given to us in the Scriptures, the real, glorified body of Jesus.

TEXT #6 **1 Cor. 15:50** "Now this I say, brethren, that flesh and blood cannot inherit the kingdom of God; neither doth corruption inherit incorruption."

Again, Paul is making the point that our bodies will be changed and be different when we are raised from the grave to eternal life. Then we will not know suffering, pain and death. Notice Paul's statements to this effect in 1 Cor. 15:52.

Our final diagram looks like this:

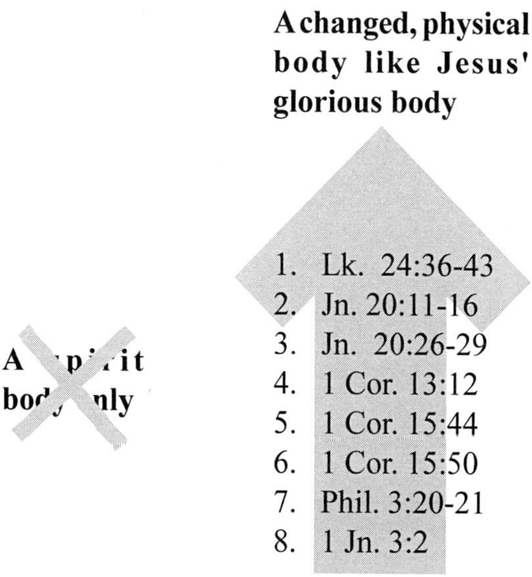

Heaven becomes much more desirable and appealing when we think of the many things that we will enjoy, as real people with real bodies that know no pain, sorrow, or death.

Ask Yourself

1. Can a spirit body build a house or plant a vineyard? Does it need a house or a vineyard? TEXT #9 of our first list says that we will do that.

2. Do spirit animals or humans need to eat? In Isa. 65:25, Phil. 3:20-21, 1 Jn. 3:2, and Lk. 24:36-43, we find that both humans and animals will eat in heaven.

3. Do spirit bodies need to grow up? In TEXT #14 of our first list it says that we will do just that.

4. Was the resurrected body of Jesus real enough for the disciples to handle and touch? (See Lk. 24:36-43 on p. 62.)

The Rapture

Most evangelical Christians believe in the second coming of Jesus and would say with Paul that they are "Looking for that blessed hope and the glorious appearing of...Jesus Christ." (Titus 2:13) The second coming of Jesus is mentioned over 300 times in the 260 chapters of the N. T.. Anyone who lines up a few texts of Scripture knows that the current world events tell us that the second coming of Jesus is to happen **soon**! (For the nearness of His coming, look up the following and compare them with current events in the world. Mt. 24; James 5:1-5; 2 Tim. 3:1-5)

In our study on the second coming of Jesus, we will not deal with whether or not Jesus will come again, or the nearness of His coming, as these are too plain to deny. But we will focus on **how Jesus will come**. This may seem very basic, but you may receive a wide range of answers from different Christians. One Christian will explain His coming one way and another just the opposite. Both will quote verses from the Bible to back their views. How will Jesus come?

There are two basic views in the Christian world today which are exclusive and contradictory.

1. The Rapture, or Secret Rapture

The details of this popular view differ in various parts of the country, but when a person speaks of "the rapture," he is indicating a belief in the following:

1. Believers are "raptured," or snatched away silently, secretly, and suddenly disappear, as Christ takes them to heaven to be with Him.

2. After the believers are "raptured away," the remaining people, called the wicked, are left alive on the earth for seven years, to face the period of tribulation and the rule of the anti-christ and the beast.

3. After the wicked have been on the earth for seven years, then Jesus returns with the believers and rules on the earth for 1000 years.

If the "rapture" teaching is diagramed on a time line, it looks something like this:

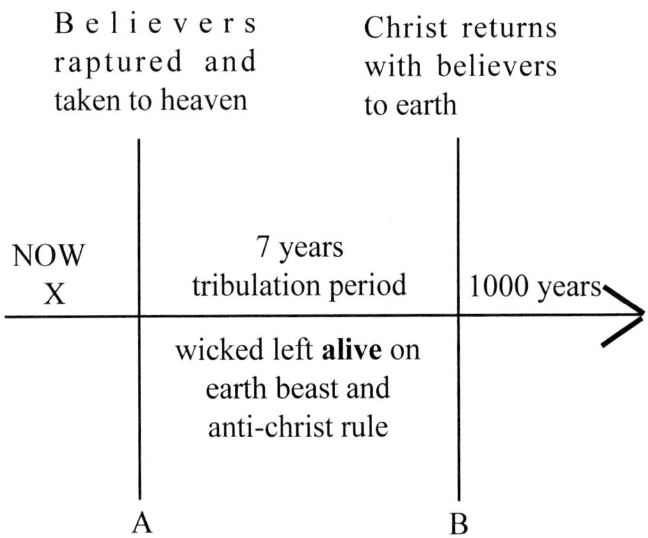

2. The Second Coming

Those who believe in the second coming, believe that Jesus will come literally. There is no room for the "secret rapture" idea, as Christ **is seen by everyone** when

He returns. At that time, the wicked are destroyed, the believers are taken to heaven, and the earth is left empty and void. There is no seven-year period of time, during which the wicked are left alive on earth, and the "A" and "B" of the above chart are one and the same event. The other significant difference in this teaching is that the "period of tribulation" happens **before** the second coming of Jesus. Diagramed, it looks like this:

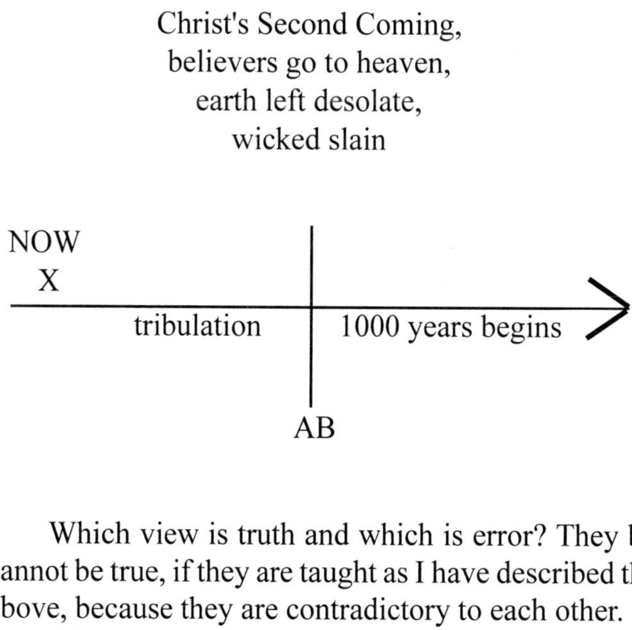

Which view is truth and which is error? They both cannot be true, if they are taught as I have described them above, because they are contradictory to each other.

When Jesus spoke to His disciples about His second coming, the first thing that He said to them was, "...take heed that no man deceive you." (Matt. 24:4) Apparently Jesus knew that there would be great confusion in the last days about His coming, and today **there is** great confusion in this area.

We could focus upon many areas in the study of "The second coming" or "the rapture," but we will zero in on the question, **How** will Jesus come?

Literal, visible Second Coming, no secret rapture, wicked slain

Secret rapture, wicked are left alive on earth

1. **Psm. 50:3-5** "Our God shall come, and...**not keep silence**: a fire shall devour before him, and it shall be very tempestuous round about him. He shall call to the heavens from above, and to the earth, that he may judge his people..."

2. **Mt. 13:37-43** Jesus comes at the end of this world, with His angels and gathers the **wicked first** (Mt. 13:30) and **then** the righteous.

3. **Mt. 16:27** He comes in His Father's glory with His angels.

4. **Mt. 24:23** "Then if any man shall say unto you, Lo, here *is* Christ, or there; **believe *it* not**."

5. **Mt. 24:26** "...if they shall say... Behold, he is in the desert; go not forth: behold, *he is* in the secret chambers; **believe *it* not.**"

Literal, visible Second Coming, no secret rapture, wicked slain

↑ 6. **Mt. 24:27** "For as the lightning cometh out of the east, and shineth even unto the west; so shall also the coming of the Son of man be."

↑ 7. **Mt. 24:30** "...then shall all the tribes of the earth mourn, and they shall **see** the Son of man coming in the clouds of heaven with power and great glory."

Secret rapture, wicked are left alive on earth

↑ 8. **Mt. 24:31** "And he shall send his angels with a great **sound of a trumpet**, and...gather together his elect..."

↑ 9. **Mt. 24:37-39** "But as the days of Noe *were*, so shall also the coming of the Son of man be..."

← 10. **Mt. 24:40-41** "Then shall two be in the field; the one shall be taken, and the other left..."

← 11. **Mt. 24:42-44** Jesus will come as a thief in the night; so be ready.

Literal, visible Second Coming, no secret rapture, wicked slain

12. **Mt. 25:31** "When the Son of man shall come in his glory, and all the holy angels with him, then shall he sit upon the throne of his glory."

13. **Mt. 26:64** "...Hereafter shall ye **see** the Son of man sitting on the right hand of power, and coming in the clouds of heaven."

Secret rapture, wicked are left alive on earth

14. **Mk. 13:21** "And then if any man shall say to you, Lo, here *is* Christ; or, lo, *he is* there; **believe *him* not**:"

15. **Mk. 13:26-27** "And then shall they **see** the Son of man coming in the clouds with great power and glory. And then shall he send his angels, and shall gather together his elect...of the earth..."

16. **Mk. 14:62** "...and **ye shall see** the Son of man sitting on the right hand of power, and coming in the clouds of heaven."

Literal, visible Second Coming, no secret rapture, wicked slain

Secret rapture, wicked are left alive on earth

17. **Lk. 12:39-40** Jesus' coming is likened to a thief; "be ready."

18. **Lk. 17:23-24** "And they shall say to you, See here; or, see there: go not after *them*, nor follow *them*. For as the lightning, that lighteneth out of the one part under heaven, shineth unto the other *part* under heaven; so shall also the Son of man be in his day."

19. **Lk. 17:26-30** "And as it was in the days of Noe, so shall it be also in the days of the Son of man."

20. **Lk. 17:34-36** "...two *men* in one bed; the one shall be taken, and the other shall be left...two men shall be in the field; the one shall be taken, and the other left."

21. **Lk. 21:27-28** "...then shall they **see** the Son of man coming in a cloud, with power and great glory...then look up, and lift up your heads; for your redemption draweth nigh."

Literal, visible Second Coming, no secret rapture, wicked slain

↑

(22.) **Acts 1:9-12** "...while they beheld, he was taken up; and a cloud received him out of their sight...this same Jesus, which is taken up from you into heaven, shall so come **in like manner** as ye have seen him go into heaven."

Secret rapture, wicked are left alive on earth

←(23.) **1 Cor. 15:52** "In a moment, in the twinkling of an eye, at the last **trump**: for the **trumpet** shall **sound**, and the dead shall be raised..."

↑

(24.) **1 Thess. 4:16-17** "For the Lord himself shall descend from heaven with a **shout**, with the voice of the archangel, and with the **trump** of God: and the dead in Christ shall rise first:" Then the saints alive on earth are caught up to "meet the Lord in the air..."

←(25.) **1 Thess. 5:2-6** Jesus comes as a thief, catches the wicked not ready, but **the righteous are not caught off guard.**

Literal, visible Second Coming, no secret rapture, wicked slain

26. **2 Thess. 1:7-10** "...when the Lord Jesus shall be revealed from heaven with his mighty angels, in flaming fire taking vengeance on them that know not God, and that obey not the gospel of our Lord Jesus Christ...When he shall come to be glorified in his saints..."

Secret rapture, wicked are left alive on earth

27. **2 Pet. 3:10** "But the day of the Lord will come as a thief in the night; in the which the heavens shall pass away with a **great noise**, and the elements shall melt with fervent heat, the earth also and the works that are therein shall be burned up."

28. **Jude 14-15** Jesus comes with His "saints" or "holy ones" to execute judgment.

29. **Rev. 1:7** "...he cometh with clouds; and **every eye shall see** him..."

As I stated before, the further we delve into some subjects, the more complex they get. Some of the texts above clearly back one view over the other. Other texts are not so clear and could lend support to either view. Let us state the clear ideas first and summarize the results.

Literal, visible Second Coming, no secret rapture, wicked slain

Jesus' 2nd coming is in the clouds of heaven, and is very visible.		Jesus' 2nd coming includes noise, like a shout or trumpet; definitely **not silent.**	Jesus comes with all the angels.
#1	#15	#1	#2
#3	#16	#8	#3
#4	#18	#20	#8
#5	#21	#21	#12
#6	#22	#24	#15
#7	#24	#27	#26
#8	#26		#28
#12	#27		
#13	#28		
#14	#29		

Next let us look at the support for the rapture view. Notice the two main ideas that the texts fit into.

The secret rapture, wicked left alive on earth

Christ's 2nd coming likened to a thief		One taken, and the other left
#11	#25	#10
#17	#27	#20

The texts that give support to the rapture idea are in the minority so let us look at their context.

To those who support the rapture idea, the term "thief" means three things: **silent, secret**, and **unexpected.** But, **did Jesus imply** that His coming would be **silent, secret**, and **unexpected**, when He used the "thief" illustration? The context surrounding the thief illustration will be enlightening and help us to understand the true meaning that Jesus attaches to the term "thief" when He uses it.

Texts that refer to the Lord's coming as "a thief in the night"

Mt. 24:43
Lk. 12:39-41
1 Thess. 5:2
2 Pet. 3:10
Rev. 3:3
Rev. 16:15

There are a total of six texts that use the phrase "a thief in the night." As we compare them, look to see if they give support to **all three words** so often associated with the thief idea (silent, secret, and unexpected).

TEXT #11 Mt. 24:43

The verses immediately before and after vs. 43 seem to go back to the **unexpected** idea. In the context of Mt. 24, Jesus specifically states that His coming will **not be secret** (Mt. 24:23, 26). There are **trumpets sounding** and angels attending His second coming. (Mt. 24:30-31) In the same chapter where Jesus likens His coming to a "thief," there are many of His statements indicating His coming will not be silent, but very visible.

The verse immediately following the thief term (vs. 44) implies the **unexpectedness** of Christ's return. It states, "...be.. ready, for in such an hour as ye think not the Son of man cometh." **If** that, indeed, means that Christ's coming will be silent and secret, the only support for that would be the phrase "one shall be taken, and the other left" (vs. 40, 41). If these verses are indicating silence, it would be contradictory not only to the verses immediately preceding and following the "thief phrase," but also to all the other evidence in Mt. 24. We will look at the context of the "one taken and the other left" phrase in a moment.

TEXT #17 Lk. 12:39-41

The context of this verse also gives support to the **unexpectedness** of Jesus' return. Note carefully that Peter was present when Jesus made the statement about His coming being like "a thief in the night" (Lk. 12:41). Peter later wrote about this very phrase and gave us important insights into the exact meaning that the Master put in the phrase. Again note, it is important that Peter was present when the "thief phrase" was used by Jesus.

Nowhere in the context of this statement does it even hint that Jesus' coming will be silent or secret.

TEXT #25 1 Thess. 5:2-6

Verse 3 gives support to the **unexpectedness** of Jesus return and says some will not be ready. Verse 4 states that the Christians should not be caught off guard or surprised by Jesus' coming, because they should be looking for it and be ready. Nowhere in this verse or in its surrounding context, can we find any support to the idea of Jesus' coming being silent or secret as in the rapture teaching.

TEXT #27 2 Pet. 3:10

In this verse, Peter gives us great insight into Jesus' statement when he likened His coming to "a thief in the night." Peter says same thing that he heard Jesus say in Lk. 12:39. He then goes on to tell us the details of what will happen when Jesus comes. It is here that we learn the true meaning of the phrase, "a thief in the night." Will it be **silent**? **Secret**? Or **unexpected**? Let Peter tell us what he heard Jesus say in Lk. 12:39-41.

Peter states, "But the day of the Lord will come as a thief in the night; in the which the heavens shall pass away **with a great noise**," (That does not sound too silent.) "and the elements shall melt with fervent heat, and the earth also and the works that are therein **shall be burned up**." (That does not appear to be too secretive, either.) Peter rules out the possibility of the term "thief" meaning silent or secret in any way. The only connotation that is left is **unexpected**. The second coming will catch many off guard because they have failed to yield to the influence of the Holy Spirit and be converted to Christ. **Thank you, Peter,** for the insights!

Rev. 3:3 and Rev. 16:15	Both verses give support to the unexpectedness of Christ's 2nd coming

If we were to use the ABC method on this subtopic and diagram our findings on the true meaning of "a thief in the night," then our diagram would look like this:

"A Thief In the Night"

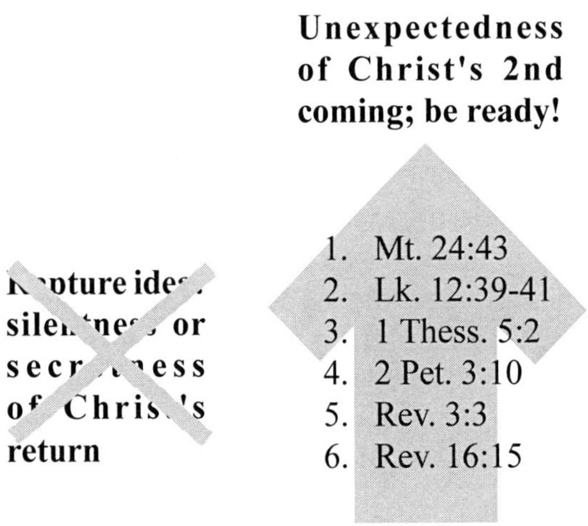

The second idea that appears to give support to the rapture teaching is that of "One taken and the other left." This phrase is often quoted by those who believe that the righteous are taken or snatched away, without warning, leaving the wicked alone on the earth. This is all supposed to happen "in the twinkling of an eye," and then Christ's believers are gone. Let us **take a closer look** at the texts that contain the phrase, "One shall be taken and the other left" to see if they really are out of line with Christ's other statements on this subject.

One taken and the other left

1. Mt. 24:40-41

2. Lk. 17:34-36

TEXT #10 Mt. 24:40-41

Immediately preceding the above statement, Jesus used the illustration of Noah and the inhabitants of the antediluvian world. He tells how **they were caught off guard**. If we analyze His illustration carefully, we will gain two interesting insights. The first is how the flood came unexpectedly and caught many in a state of unpreparedness. So the coming of the Son of man will catch many in that same state of unpreparedness.

Secondly, Jesus said Mt. 24:37, "But as the days of Noah *were*, so shall also the coming of the Son of man be." In the story of Noah the **taken** ones are **not** the righteous but the **wicked**! Note Mt. 24:38-39 in the following translations.

KJV "For as in the days that were before the flood they [the wicked, or unprepared] were eating and...knew not until the flood came, and **took** them all away..."

NIV "For in the days before the flood, **people** were eating and...they knew nothing about what would happen until the flood came and **took** them all away."

NAB "In the days before the flood **people** were eating and...They were totally unconcerned until the flood came and **destroyed** them."

According to the rapture teaching, it is the saints that are the ones **taken** and the wicked are the ones **left**. This is the opposite of how Jesus used the illustration of Noah. Also, in the rapture view, the wicked are left alive on the earth but in Jesus' illustration the wicked are destroyed. "As the days of Noah were, so shall also the coming of the Son of man be." Note the chart below:

The Bible teaches

The Taken are the wicked.
The Left are the Righteous.
The wicked are destroyed

Rapture teaching

The Taken are the Righteous. The Left are the Wicked. The wicked are left alive

1. KJV
2. NEB
3. NAB

Which is truth? Which is error? It becomes easier to tell as we go along. More and more parts of the puzzle begin to fall into place and the picture gets clearer and clearer.

The "thief idea" immediately follows Mt. 24:40-41. According to our last study and Peter's first hand witness, this phrase emphasizes the **unexpectedness** of Christ's return. In Peter's use of the "thief phrase" (2 Pet. 3:10), he tells of the total destruction of the world and everything in it and around it. **This would leave no room for the rapture interpretation that the wicked are left alive on the earth for seven years**. The wicked being destroyed not only fits Peter's interpretation of the "thief phrase," but also Christ's illustration of Noah!

Since the "thief" concept is very much a part of the immediate context of our "one taken and the other left," we must take that into consideration when interpreting this passage. When we take into consideration the context before and after Mt. 24, we must conclude that Christ's return **will not be silent or secret**. The phrase, "one taken and the other left:, must mean that one person is ready, and the other is not. Only God knows who is ready and who is not. For all intents and purposes, we cannot tell from the outward appearance, but God looks on the heart.

TEXT #20 Lk. 17:34-36

The verses immediately preceding this statement emphasize two things: First, the **unexpectedness** of Christ's return and that the wicked will be **unprepared**; secondly, the same analysis of who are **taken** and who are **left**. See the study in this chapter that we just finished on TEXT #10 for further details. When studying the context of any verse, it is always a good idea to read the verse immediately preceding and following the text. The verse that follows Lk. 17:34-36 will give us **great help**. Look at it closely.

Lk. 17:37 "And they [the disciples] answered and said unto him, Where, Lord? And he said unto them, Wheresoever the body *is*, thither will the eagles [or vultures] be gathered together."

Notice Jesus' words in some modern translations. It will help to clarify His answer.

NIV "Where there is a **dead body**, there the **vultures** will gather."

NEB "Where the **corpse** is, there the **vultures** will gather."

Phillips "Wherever there is a **dead body**, there the **vultures** will flock."

NAB "Wherever the **carcass** is, there will the **vultures** gather."

It is quite obvious that Jesus was speaking of dead bodies and vultures, not eagles. That issue, if left unstated, might detract from the real issue here. The disciples could have been asking the question one of two ways:

"Where will the taken ones be taken?"

"Where will the left ones be left?"

Consider the disciples' question and the answer that

Jesus gave to them **in light of the rapture interpretation.** See if that view can be correct according to the context.

If the disciples were asking the question this way:

"Where will the taken ones be taken?"

What would be the ramifications in light of Jesus' answer? The rapture interpretation says the "taken ones" are taken to heaven to be with Jesus. Jesus' answer indicates that **they were taken to destruction** where the dead bodies are and the vultures gather. The rapture view apparently would be incorrect and contradictory if the disciples were asking the question as stated above. Maybe the disciples were not asking, "Where will the taken ones be taken?" But instead, maybe they were asking, "Where will the left ones be left?" Let us look at the other possibility and give the "rapture view" the benefit of the doubt.

If the disciples were asking:

"Where will the left ones be left?"

Jesus' answer would then be that **the ones left are dead and slain** because they are dead bodies where the vultures gather. This would go along with the "rapture idea" of the "taken ones" being the righteous but would contradict the rapture teaching that the wicked are left alive on the earth after the rapture. **According to the answer that Jesus gave, neither way of understanding the rapture view fits the Scriptural context of the verse.** By studying the context of this one verse, we can easily tell that **the rapture view cannot be correct.**

Notice, though, that Jesus' answer does go back to the idea that Peter gives (2 Pet. 3:10) when he states that the whole world and all the works that are therein will be **burned up** when Jesus comes as "a thief in the night."

There is perfect harmony in the Word of God when we take it as it is, in its simplicity, without twisting and interpreting. According to Jesus, He will come in the clouds with all His angels. Every eye will see Him (Rev. 1:7), the wicked will be destroyed, and the righteous will return to heaven where Jesus has prepared a place for them. (Jn. 14:1-3) Jesus also states that the wicked will be the **first ones taken** (Mt. 13:30) and will be destroyed by the brightness of His coming (2 Thess. 1:9; 2:8). They will cry for the rocks and the mountains to fall on them and hide them from the face of the lamb (Rev. 6:14-17).

A diagram of the two texts, Mt. 24:40-41 and Lk. 17:34-36, looks like this:

"One taken and the other left"
(from context alone)

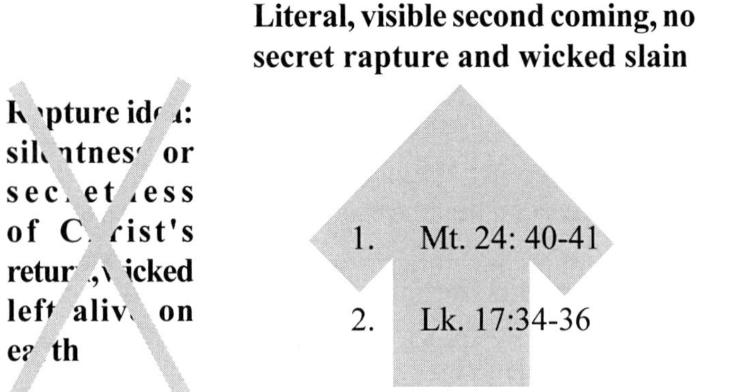

After taking a closer look at the two ideas that give support to the "rapture teaching," the earnest Christian can easily tell that there **is no support** in the Scriptures for that teaching.

The rapture teaches that there will be a second chance for people to repent and be converted during the tribulation. First of all, Rev. 16:8-11 states twice that there is no repentance taking place during the tribulation. Secondly, 2 Peter 3:10 leaves no room for the view that anyone is left alive on the earth to be converted after the thief in the night, as "the earth also and the works that are therein shall be burned up." Thirdly, Heb. 9:27 states, "It is appointed unto men once to die, but after this the judgement." No second chance!

In addition to the two main concepts (thief, and one taken...) that are usually quoted as giving support to the rapture, I have heard other texts used.

The first is 1 Cor. 15:52 (TEXT #23). It is often quoted to show that the rapture will happen quickly, in the twinkling of an eye. When this text is analyzed in light of its context and the Big Picture, then you begin to notice other parts of the text. Notice that a change takes place in God's people, ***at* the sound of the trumpet**. We will put on immortality and be changed, but it is **no secret!** Surely it is not **silent** with the **trumpet blasting!** This must be the same trumpet that awakens the dead to life (1 Th. 4:16-17) and is mentioned in Mt. 24:31 when God's angels gather the saints from the earth, and Jesus is **seen by all,** coming in the clouds of heaven.

The trumpet is important because it signals the angels to gather the saints from the earth (Mt. 24:31). How 1 Cor. 15:52 can ever be used to back the silent, secret rapture, with the trumpet blasting, I will never know!

These three texts listed below will help to illustrate that the three texts are referring to one event, not two events separated by seven years of tribulation.

The Second Coming, literal and visible

1. **Mt. 24:30-31** "And then shall **appear** the sign of the Son of man **in heaven**: and then shall **all the tribes of the earth mourn**, and **they shall see** the Son of man coming in the clouds of heaven with power and great glory. And he shall send his angels **with a great sound of a trumpet**, and they shall gather together his elect..."

2. **1 Cor. 15:52** "In a moment, in the twinkling of an eye, at the last **trump**: for the **trumpet shall sound**, and the dead shall be raised incorruptible, and we shall be changed."

3. **1 Thess. 4:16** "For the Lord himself shall descend from heaven **with a shout**, with the voice of the archangel, and with the **trump** of God: and the dead in Christ shall rise first:"

Notice in all three scriptures that there is a **trumpet sounding** and the righteous are being gathered. The rapture teaching does not recognize that the above three texts are referring to **one** event. It teaches that TEXT #2 refers to a separate event that happens seven years before the events described in TEXT #1 (A and B on the chart p. 68). After close examination and comparison of these three scriptures, **it is abundantly clear** that they are all referring to **one event** and **not two,** separated by seven years of tribulation.

The only other text I have ever heard used in defense of the rapture is Jude 14 and 15 (TEXT #28). This text tells about Jesus returning to this earth **with** His saints. It is often quoted to prove that the saints have to be raptured away before the literal, visible coming of Jesus because the saints are mentioned in the text **as returning with Christ** when He comes the second time. The word in question is translated "saints" in the KJV. Notice how it is translated in **all** of the newer translations:

Jude 14

NIV "...the Lord is coming with thousands upon thousands of his **holy ones**..."

NEB "I saw the Lord come with the **myriads of angels**..."

Phillips "...the Lord came with ten thousand of his **holy ones**..."

NAB "...Lord has come with his countless **holy ones** about him."

The word translated "saints" in the KJV has caused much confusion. The word from the Greek should have been translated "holy ones," as the newer translations show, and **not** "saints." Notice that the NEB version of the Bible translated the word as "angels," which fits the Big Picture in God's Word. This reference (Jude 14 and 15) has apparently led thousands to think that the rapture idea was true because the translators of the KJV in 1611 decided to translate the Greek "saints" instead of "holy ones."

If this text is translated "saints," it is then in contradiction with the rest of the texts on this subject. If it is translated "holy ones," then it fits harmoniously with all of the references that say Christ will come with His angels. (See chart on p. 76.)

We do not have to invent theories and ideas to have Christ coming for His believers silently and secretly so that He then can come back with them, as a superficial reading of this text might indicate. If Jude 14-15 were the only light and information on this subject, we could still look at the Greek of this text and figure it out. But Jude **is not the only source of light we have** on this subject!

The view of the literal, visible coming of Christ may not be as popular as "the rapture" view, but remember, the popularity of a certain teaching **does not make it true**. Jesus stands on the side of **truth** (His Word) and does not contradict Himself.

Ask Yourself

1. Does the Bible specifically say that the righteous will pass through the tribulation? Note Rev. 7:13-14 in some various translations.

   KJV "...What are these which are arrayed in white robes? and whence came they?...These are they which **came out of great tribulation**, and have washed their robes, and made them white in the blood of the lamb." (Can you come out of something if you have not been in it?)

   Phillips "...these are they that have **come though** the great oppression..."

   NEB "...these are the men that **have passed through** the great ordeal..."

NAB "...these are the ones that **have survived** the great period of trial..."

You can find many other verses in the New and Old Testament that speak clearly about the righteous going through the "time of trouble or tribulation" with God being their protection through it all. (See Psm. 37:19, 39-40; Psm. 50:15; Psm. 91; Prov. 12:13; Isa. 1:25; Isa. 26:20-21; Dan. 3; Mal. 3:2-3; 1 Cor. 3:13; 1 Pet. 1:6-7; 1 Pet. 4:12.)

2. Does Jesus specifically connect the time of His coming (when one is taken and the other left), with the time when the wicked are slain? (See Lk. 17:34-37. A quick look in a concordance, at the words "slain", "vultures", and "dead bodies", will connect many other scriptures and events with the second coming of Jesus.)

3. Are the texts that support the literal, visible Second Coming in the majority?

4. Does Peter say that when the Lord comes as a "thief in the night," the earth will be burned up (2 Pet. 3:10)?

5. Was Peter present when Jesus used the term "thief" to describe His second coming (Lk. 12:39-41)?

6. Is it safe to assume that there is no room for the wicked to be left alive on the earth after Jesus returns **if the earth is burned up** (2 Pet. 3:10)?

7. Carefully compare 1 Cor. 15:52; 1 Thess. 4:16-17; and Mt. 24:30-31. Is there a trumpet sounding in each of these texts?

8. Are the three texts mentioned in #7 referring to one event? Those who teach the rapture would lead you to believe that two of the texts speak of the same event, and the other (Mt. 24:30-31) tells of an event to take place seven years later.

A Time Line to Illustrate Truth

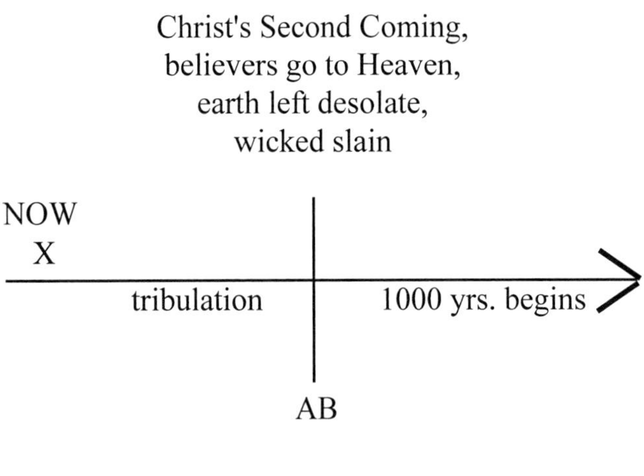

Our final diagram looks like this:

Literal, visible Second Coming, no secret rapture, wicked slain

1. Psm. 50:3-5
2. Mt. 13:37-43
3. Mt. 16:27
4. Mt. 24:23
5. Mt. 24:26
6. Mt. 24:27
7. Mt. 24:30
8. Mt. 24:31
9. Mt. 24:37-39
10. Mt. 24:40-41
11. Mt. 24:42-44
12. Mt. 25:31
13. Mt. 26:64
14. Mk. 13:21
15. Mk. 13:26-27
16. Mk. 14:62
17. Lk. 12:39-41
18. Lk. 17:23-24
19. Lk. 17:26-30
20. Lk. 17:34-36
21. Lk. 21:27-28
22. Acts 1:9-11
23. 1 Cor. 15:52
24. 1 Thess. 4:16-17
25. 1 Thess. 5:2-6
26. 2 Thess. 1:7-10
27. 2 Pet. 3:10
28. Jude 14, 15
29. Rev. 1:7

Secret rapture, wicked are left alive on earth

The rapture teaching that the tribulation occurs **after** the second coming, and not before, may cause some believers to lose their salvation for the following reasons:

1. Lack of Preparation.

Each day we should be **learning to live by faith**, asking God for our needs and depending more and more on Him to provide. **Many talk faith** but do not know what it means to claim God's promises and **expect** Him to deliver. When the events of the tribulation begin to transpire and the "mark of the beast" is enforced, food and earnings will be cut off from the righteous (Rev. 13:15-17), and they will be forced to lean upon God. God has promised to provide bread and water for the righteous in their hour of need (Isa. 33:16). If the righteous were snatched away and did not go through the time of trouble (tribulation), then what preparation would they have to make? God wants people who will not only talk faith but be willing to live by **faith alone**! It is clear that God purifies His people by bringing them **through** hard times. In this process, likened to the purifying of metal, God separates the dross from the gold. (See Psm. 11:5-6; 66:10; Is. 1:25; 48:10; Jer. 6:27-29; Zech 13:9; Mal 3:2-3; 1 Cor. 3:13.)

2. Possibility of Being Deceived.

If there are false prophets and teachers on the earth now, as the Bible says there will be before the Second Coming (Mt. 24:4-5, 24), there is a strong chance that many might be following a false teacher **now**. They may not even think to test that teacher's words against God's Word, and therefore **they will be deceived**. Also, if a person expects the beast to come on the scene of action **after** the Second Coming and not before, then that person will not be looking for a correct understanding of the beast or his mark. They may make the beast out to be a **fanciful creature of the future**, who needs not to be reckoned with now! Thus many might receive the mark of the beast and not realize it until it is too late.

Hell

Hell is one of the most confusing subjects because words in the KJV that are translated "hell" do not mean hell. There are four different words translated hell. Only one of them clearly means **the place of punishment** that we normally think of when we speak of hell. Here is a list of the words translated hell and their true meaning.

1. **Tartaroo**: (Greek verb) Appears only once in the entire Bible; so its exact meaning is hard for translators to pin down. It is found in 2 Pet. 2:4 and means "a place where divine punishment was meted out."

2. **Hades**: (Greek) means **grave**.

3. **Sheol**: (Hebrew) means **grave**.

4. **Gehenna:**(Greek) means a place of punishment.
   Mt. 5:22, 29-30
   Mt. 10:28; 18:9, 23:33
   Mk. 9:43, 45, 47

As in many other subjects of the Bible, at first glance, it seems there are two very differing views in the Scriptures. The subject of "Hell" is no exception.

1. **The fires of hell burn on and on without end, and torment goes on forever and ever through eternity. (This view has caused many sincere people to say, "If that is what**

a loving God is all about, then I want no part of religion.")

2. **The fires of Hell do burn, but will eventually go out when they have totally destroyed the wicked.**

Both views cannot be true. Either the fires burn on and on, or they go out. If God was saying both views are correct, then He would be contradicting Himself. We know that God cannot lie; therefore one view **must** be true and the other erroneous. But which is which? Let us line up the texts.

The fires of Hell eventually go out, wicked destroyed and become ashes

↑

(1.) **Psm. 37:20** "But the wicked shall **perish**, and the enemies of the LORD *shall be* as the fat of lambs: they shall **consume; into smoke** shall they **consume away**."

↑

Hell burns on and on without end forever

(2.) **Isa 47:14** "Behold, they shall be **as stubble**; the fire shall burn them; they shall not deliver themselves from the power of the flame: *there shall* **not** *be* a coal to warm at, *nor* fire to sit before it."

The fires of Hell eventually go out, wicked destroyed and become ashes

Hell burns on and on without end forever

3.) **Isa. 66:24** "...for their worm shall not die, neither shall their fire be quenched..."

4.) **Eze. 18:4, 20** "...the **soul** that sinneth, **it shall die**..."

5.) **Mal. 4:1, 3** "For, behold, the day cometh, that shall burn as an oven; and all the proud, yea, and all that do wickedly, shall be stubble: and the day that cometh shall **burn them up**, saith the LORD of hosts, that it shall leave them neither root nor branch....for they shall be **ashes** under the soles of your feet in the day that I shall do *this*, saith the LORD of hosts."

6.) **Mt. 3:12** "...he will **burn up** the chaff with unquenchable fire."

7.) **Mt. 7:13-14** "Enter ye in at the strait gate: for wide *is* the gate, and broad *is* the way, that leadeth to destruction..."

The fires of Hell eventually go out, wicked destroyed and become ashes

← 8. **Mt. 18:8** "...it is better for thee to enter into life halt or maimed, rather than having two hands or two feet to be cast into everlasting fire."

← 9. **Mt. 25:46** "And these shall go away into everlasting punishment: But the righteous into life eternal."

Hell burns on and on without end forever

← 10. **Mk. 9:43-44** "...it is better for thee to enter into life maimed, than having two hands to go into hell, into the fire that never shall be quenched. Where their worm dieth not, and the fire is not quenched."

↑ 11. **Jn. 3:16** "For God so loved the world, that he gave his only begotten Son, that whosoever believeth in him should not **perish**..."

↑ 12. **Rom. 6:23** "...the wages of sin is **death**; but the gift of God is eternal life through Jesus Christ our Lord."

The fires of Hell eventually go out, wicked destroyed and become ashes

13. **2 Thess. 1:7-10** When the Lord comes with his mighty angels, the wicked "...shall be punished with everlasting destruction from the presence of the Lord, and from the glory of his power..."

14. **2 Pet. 2:6** "And turning the cities of Sodom and Gomorrah into **ashes**...making them an ensample unto those that after should live ungodly."

Hell burns on and on without end forever

15. **2 Pet. 3:7, 10** "But the heavens and the earth, which are now, by the same word are kept in store, reserved unto fire against the day of judgment and perdition of ungodly men. But the day of the Lord will come as a thief in the night;...the earth also and the works that are therein shall be **burned up**."

16. **Jude 7** "Even as Sodom and Gomorrah...are set forth for an example, suffering the vengeance of **eternal fire**."

The fires of Hell eventually go out, wicked destroyed and become ashes

17. **Rev. 20:9** "...and fire came down from God out of heaven, and **devoured** them."

Hell burns on and on without end forever

18. **Rev. 20:10** "And the devil that deceived them was cast into the lake of fire and brimstone...and shall be tormented day and night for ever and ever."

19. **Rev. 20:14** "And death and hell were cast into the lake of fire. This is the second **death**.

The subject of hell is, without question, one of the most difficult and perplexing studies, because there seems to be such strong support for both views. But if we stick to our original assumption that God does not lie and contradict Himself, then we will find an answer that will show that God's Word is not confused.

The key to the subject of Hell is not as readily available as some of the other subjects that we have studied; so we must dig a little deeper to find it. The careful student will find that the key is in the context, though. You do not have to look far to find the apparent contradictions in this subject for they are even found in the same verse. Read carefully Jesus' statement in Mt. 3:12.

"...but he will **burn up** the chaff with **unquenchable fire**."

You would think that if a person were **burned up** he would be destroyed and gone. However, the next line indicates that it is an **unquenchable** fire. Can both parts of the verse be accurate? On the surface it appears that the two terms are not compatible. Either being **burned up** does not mean destroyed and gone (TEXTS #1, 2, 4, 5, 7, 11, 12, 13, 14, 15, 16, 17, 19), or **unquenchable fire** does not mean fire that goes on forever without end (TEXTS #8, 9, 18).

Below, I have summarized our findings.

Hell burns on and on without end forever	**The fires of Hell eventually go out, wicked destroyed and become ashes**	
#3	#1	#12
#6*	#2	#13*
#8	#4	#14
#9	#5	#15
#10	#6*	#16
#13*	#7	#17
#18	#11	#19

* these texts have parts that fit in both.

There are two main areas or headings that the minority of texts seem to fit into, and they are as follows:

1. Unquenchable fire (TEXTS #3, 6, 10)

2. Everlasting or eternal punishment (TEXTS #8, 9, 18)

As we look at TEXT #3, we will also look at TEXT #6 and 10. All three are dealing with the idea of "unquenchable fire."

TEXT #3 **Isa. 66:24** "And they shall go forth, and look upon the carcasses of the men that have transgressed against me: for their worm shall not die, neither shall their fire be quenched; and they shall be an abhorring unto all flesh."

TEXT #6 **Mt. 3:12** "...but he will burn up the chaff with unquenchable fire."

TEXT #10 **Mk. 9:43-44** "...it is better for thee to enter into life maimed, than having two hands to go into hell, into the fire that never shall be quenched: Where their worm dieth not, and the fire is not quenched."

We normally think that the term **unquenchable fire** means fire that never goes out. However, in the Bible and also today, we have fires that are **unquenchable,** but that does **not** mean that they never go out!

The Biblical usage of the term **unquenchable** becomes abundantly clear when we read Jeremiah's prophecy about Jerusalem. Jeremiah said that if God's people did not stop trampling on the Sabbath, then Jerusalem would be "**devoured**" with a fire that "**shall not be quenched**," in Jeremiah 17:27.

The fulfillment of Jeremiah's prophecy is recorded in 2 Chronicles 36:19-21, where it plainly states that the palaces of Jerusalem were burnt with fire (vs. 19) "...to fulfil the Word of the Lord by the mouth of Jeremiah..." (vs. 21).

I would ask you, **Is Jerusalem still burning today**? **No**! Of course not! So according to the Bible the term **unquenchable** does **not** mean **never ending** but only that no one can put the fire out, it is **unquenchable**. If the term **unquenchable fire** meant never ending, then Jerusalem would still be burning today. Jerusalem is **not** still burning; so the term **does not mean on and on without end**. When God kindled a fire in the gates of Jerusalem, it was an **unquenchable** fire, and **no one**, but **no one**, could put it out! Notice the phrase that described this very same idea in TEXT #2 when it states:

> "...they shall not deliver themselves from the power of the flame..." but then says, "there shall not be a coal to warm at, nor fire to sit before it."

Apparently the fire in Jerusalem **did go out when it had burned up all that there was to burn!**

We have **unquenchable** fires today. Huge buildings start burning and no matter how much water is put on the flames, the fire cannot be extinquished. The fire goes out by itself **when there is nothing left to burn**, and everything is turned into **ashes**.

This understanding also gives new meaning to the texts about the wicked being **burned up** and becoming **ashes** under the soles of the feet of the righteous (TEXTS

#1, 2, 5, 13, 14, 15, 17, 19). You will notice one other thing when you begin to "rightly divide the Word of Truth." The contradictions in God's Word disappear and all of the writers' ideas harmonize so that there is greater clarity and understanding.

Since TEXTS #8, 9, and 18 all relate to the second concept of "everlasting fire or punishment," I will deal with them together.

TEXT #8 **Mt. 18:8** "...it is better for thee to enter into life halt or maimed, rather than having two hands or two feet to be cast into everlasting fire."

TEXT #9 **Mt. 25:46** "And these shall go away into everlasting punishment: but the righteous into life eternal."

TEXT #18 **Rev. 20:10** "And the devil that deceived them was cast into the lake of fire and brimstone, where the beast and the false prophet *are*, and shall be tormented day and night for ever and ever."

The key to understanding these statement comes in an apparent contradiction. Both Jude 7 and 2 Pet. 2:6 (TEXTS #16 and 14) tell about Sodom and Gomorrah. Jude clearly states that they suffered the vengeance of **eternal** fire, but 2 Pet. 2:6 says they were turned into **ashes**. Apparently the Biblical writers saw no contradiction in the terms, "reduced to ashes" and "eternal fire."

Note the diagram below which shows all the different English words that come from the same Greek root word.

This will help us to understand the apparent contradiction and help things fall into place.

Mt. 18:8	(TEXT #8)	"**EVELASTING** fire"
Mt. 25:46	(TEXT #9)	"**EVERLASTING** punishment"
2 Thess. 1:7-10	(TEXT #13)	"**EVERLASTING** destruction"
Jude 7	(TEXT #16)	"**ETERNAL** fire"
Rev. 20:10	(TEXT #18)	"For **EVER AND EVER**"

All of the capital words above come from the same Greek root word (aion). It is more than just interesting to note that it is the same root word in all of the above phrases. But the English translators chose to translate the word in many different ways. This is significant because the word used to describe the "everlasting fires" of hell is the same word as **eternal** fire used to describe the fires that destroyed Sodom and Gomorrah. In light of this, we must ask ourselves two important questions:

1. Is Sodom still burning today?

2. Is there more than one way to understand the words eternal and everlasting?

In answer to the first question, **no, Sodom and Gomorrah are not burning today**! The cities of Sodom and Gomorrah are believed to be near the southern edge of the Dead Sea. The uncompromising answer to the first question gives us a big clue as to how we should answer the second question. There is another way to understand the word "**eternal**," and "**everlasting**" and "**forever and ever**." The cities of Sodom and Gomorrah are definitely **not** still burning, as in **burning without end**, but they were **eternally destroyed** and the results of the fire were **everlasting**. Their destruction was eternal, and they were cut off "forever and ever." Remember, in order for the word **everlasting** to mean "on and on without end," Sodom would still have to be burning today!

If we take the Biblical context of these terms (everlasting, eternal, forever and ever), which means to eternally destroy something and apply this meaning to the Big Picture, we can clearly see why the Bible writers had no trouble saying that the wicked would be destroyed with eternal fire and then still say that the same wicked would be **turned into ashes** when the fires of hell go out.

Note also that in Mt. 25:46 (TEXT #9) Jesus does say that the wicked will go away into everlasting punish**ment** and **not** punish**ing**.

The reward of the wicked is eternal **death** and separation from the source of life but **not** being eternally (unendingly) punished by an unmerciful God.

TEXT #18 **Rev. 20:10** "And the devil...shall be tormented day and night for **ever and ever**."

The reason I have put this text in twice is that I think that we should look closely at the context. If we were to understand this text as saying the fires of hell burn on and on without end, then we would be making an impossible contradiction within the text itself. Notice Rev. 20:9-10 where three specific details of Hell are mentioned.

1. The devil is cast into the lake of fire.

2. The fires **devour** him.

3. The devil is tormented **forever and ever.**

How can he burn forever and ever and be devoured at the same time? It does not say that the flames enveloped him; it says they **devoured** him. Notice also vs. 14 (TEXT #19) in which it states that the fires of Hell are "the **second death**." If the devil or anyone else lives on indefinitely in the fires of hell, then **how** can it be called the second **death**? Death is the cessation of life.

Notice that similar language is used to describe the destruction of the devil in an O.T. prophecy; speaking of him in symbolic terms it says,

> "...therefore will I bring forth a fire from the midst of thee, it shall **devour** thee, and I will bring these to **ashes** upon the earth..." (Eze. 28:18).

Does he burn on and on without end, or burn up and turn into ashes? Notice the statement in the very next verse.

"...and never shalt thou be any more" (vs. 19).

Does this mean that he is destroyed and gone forever? The word translated "forever" in the Old and New Testament is used in different ways to describe different periods of time. Notice some of the ways that it can be translated.

Forever:

1. Going on and on without end
2. Exaggerated use of the word
3. As long as life shall last

Here are some examples of the different ways the Bible writers used the words "forever and ever."

1. Forever: going on and on without end

This usage can be determined by the context of the statements and the substance, person, or thing that the word describes. In 2 Cor. 9:9 it says the righteousness of God will remain "forever."

Since the word is attached to or is describing God's righteousness, and nowhere in the Scriptures is He portrayed as becoming unrighteous in the future, then it can safely be assumed that our phrase "forever and ever" carries with it the meaning of "without end."

Rev. 22:5 mentions that the saints will reign with God "forever." Since there is no contradiction in the Scriptures to indicate that the "eternal life" that Christ offers to His followers will ever end, it can safely be assumed that it means without end. There are many examples of this usage in the Bible. It is usually found referring to the traits of God that will always be continuing and unchanging, or to the life that He has promised to the redeemed.

The key to determining if this usage is referred to is this: see if **all the statements** in the Bible **agree** as to **the duration** of the event or trait. If there is nothing to indicate that it will change, then it means without end.

For further examples, see the word "forever" in any concordance.

2. Forever: exaggerated use of the words

The word "forever" is used in the Bible in an exaggerated way, just as we say sometimes, "this job will take me **forever** to accomplish." It may not take us forever, but to us, if the task is an unpleasant one, then it can seem like an eternity until it is finished.

One good example of this is found in Jonah 2:6 when Jonah was in the belly of the great fish for three days and three nights. For poor Jonah, it must have been an eternity because he speaks of this time period as being "forever."

3. Forever: as long as life shall last

In 1 Sam. 1:22, 28, we find the phrase **forever** used in this way. Here it does not mean **on and on without end**, but it means **as long as life shall last**. When Hannah took the child Samuel to the temple, she said, "...*then* I will bring him, that he may appear before the LORD, and **there abide forever**." In verse 28 she said, "Therefore also I have lent him to the LORD; **as long as he liveth** he shall be lent to the Lord...."

Another such usage can be found in Exodus 21:5-6. It speaks of a servant being set free and then not wanting to leave his master. A hole was put through his ear and it said, "he shall **serve him forever**."

I do not know of any servant in times present or past who can continue to serve his master after he is dead. So again in this example, "forever" must mean "as long as life shall last."

In Deut. 23:3, the word "forever" means ten generations. Psm. 48:14 says God will be our guide "forever and ever," but then it says He will be our guide "even **until death**." Jesus stated that God is the God of the living and not the God of the dead (Mt. 22:32; Mk. 12:27; Lk. 20:38). In the Biblical context of Psm. 48:14, it would again be comparing "forever" to "as long as life shall last."

The study of hell is one of the most difficult, and it is no wonder. There are different terms, such as "everlasting, eternal, and forever and ever," and then some different meanings to the words on top of that.

When the Big Picture is presented and various Scriptures are brought to bear on one another to ascertain their true import and meaning, then we can see that the Bible does not teach that the fires of hell burn on and on without end, showing a God who is merciless. They **do** teach that the fires of hell are real, do destroy and turn to ashes, and will go out when they have accomplished their job of burning up the wicked.

How long will they burn we are **not** told. Some parts of an unquenchable fire burn longer than others today; and some wicked, like the devil, will burn longer than others. With this understanding of the fires of hell, we could take Rom. 6:23 to mean exactly what it states, "For the wages of sin *is* **death**; but the gift of God *is* life eternal...." It does **not** say that the wages of sin is life eternal **in torment**, but **it does state** that the wages of sin is **death**.

If we back the view of hell burning on and on without end, we paint God as giving out **punishment without end** for a person's sinful existence of about 70 to 80 years. This would indicate that God finds pleasure in the death and torment of the wicked. With that view God would have to be keeping people alive because it would be by

His power that anyone could stay alive in the fires of a never-ending hell. If we were to carry this view to its ultimate end, then we again would see that we had arrived at a place in direct contradiction to the Bible. Note the following Scriptures that tell us about a loving God and the fires of hell.

> **Eze. 33:11** "...*As* I live, saith the Lord God, I have no pleasure in the death of the wicked; but that the wicked turn from his way and live..."

> **Isa. 28:21** "For the Lord shall rise up as *in* mount Perazim, he shall be wroth as *in* the valley of Gibeon, that he may do his work, his strange work; and bring to pass his act, his strange act."

If we diagram our findings from the Biblical context, our diagram looks like this:

The fires of Hell eventually go out, wicked destroyed and become ashes

1. Psm. 37:20
2. Isa. 47:14
3. Isa. 66:24
4. Eze. 18:4, 20
5. Mal. 4:1, 3
6. Mt. 3:12
7. Mt. 7:13, 14
8. Mt. 18:8
9. Mt. 25:46
10. Mk. 9:43-44
11. Jn. 3:16
12. Rom. 6:23
13. 2 Thess. 1:7-10
14. 2 Pet. 2:6
15. 2 Pet. 3:7, 10
16. Jude 7
17. Rev. 20:9
18. Rev. 20:10
19. Rev. 20:14

~~**Hell burns on and on without end forever**~~

Baptism

Baptism is a subject that has perplexed some Christians because there is much disagreement as to how and when it should take place. Some churches sprinkle newborn infants with a few drops of water and declare them baptized. Others pour water over people of any age and pronounce them baptized. Still others totally immerse people in water, **only** when the person is old enough to make his own decision to be baptized. Which is right? Which is wrong? Does it make a difference?

Our approach to this subject will be a little different from some of the subjects that we have already covered. The ABC Method of Bible Study lends itself to the study of subjects that have controversy surrounding them. The subject of baptism has some controversy around it, but that controversy does not arise out of the fact that there are Scriptural texts that "appear" to be contradicting one another.

There are texts in the Bible that tell us about baptism, what it means and when it should be performed. There are even Biblical examples for us to follow, but they are all one-sided. Usually we can find at least three or four texts in the minority to determine where an incorrect teaching originates; but with the subject of baptism, there is no such minority.

First, we will cover some items that will comprise background material in order to gain a large enough perspective for the study of this subject. Then, we will be able to find the Big picture on this subject.

ITEM #1 The Word Baptize

The Greek word **was not translated** to English but was transliterated. This means they made a new English word out of the Greek. The Greek word is **baptism** and means **to immerse,** never to pour over or sprinkle. In 1611 when the KJV was translated, the majority of the churches were not following the practice of immersing people to baptize. This transliterating of the Greek word allowed them to continue the unscriptural practice of sprinkling or pouring. After this they included all three practices under the same word, **baptism**. If you do not read Greek, you can confirm this fact in one of the following ways:

a. Ask a Greek teacher at a theological seminary.

b. Look in a Greek-English dictionary

c. Contact a Greek Orthodox Church and ask a priest what the word baptism means or what kind of baptism they perform.

ITEM #2 The Symbolic Meaning of Baptism

The meaning of baptism can quickly be ascertained because there are only two verses in the Bible that deal directly with its meaning. There is no controversy among Christians about their interpretation. They are as follows:

Rom. 6:3-4 "Know ye not, that so many of us as were baptized into Jesus Christ were baptized into his **death**? Therefore we are **buried** with him by baptism into death: that like as Christ was **raised**

up from the dead by the glory of the Father, even so we also should walk in newness of life."

Col. 2:12 "**Buried** with him in baptism, wherein also ye are **risen** with *him* through the faith of the operation of God, who hath raised him from the dead."

These two texts say that baptism is a memorial of the death, burial and resurrection of Jesus, and is symbolic of these three important events.

The Death of Jesus: It is symbolic of the death of our sinful natures when we accept Jesus as our Saviour.

The Burial of Jesus: Just as Jesus was buried in the earth, so people who accept Jesus as their personal Saviour are buried beneath the watery grave of baptism.

The Resurrection of Jesus: Just as Jesus was resurrected from the grave to new life, so the follower of Christ is raised from the watery grave of baptism to walk in newness of life in Christ.

We can easily see from the symbolism of baptism that it is best represented by one method: **baptism by immersion**. How can sprinkling represent the burial of Christ when the person who is being baptized is never buried in the watery grave? Baptizing in any other way loses much of the meaning built into the term.

According to other verses in the N.T., a person's sins are washed away when he is baptized. Note these verses.

Acts 2:38 "Then Peter said unto them, Repent, and be baptized every one of you in the name of Jesus Christ **for the remission of sins**..."

Acts 22:16 "And now why tarriest thou? arise, and be baptized, and **wash away thy sins**, calling on the name of the Lord."

The symbolic meaning of baptism is very much the same in all churches. The method that the church uses (sprinkling, pouring or immersion) is varied and differs from church to church. This is what we will focus our study upon. The two different views are stated below.

The First View: There is no preparation necessary for baptism. It is something that should be done and the obligation rests upon the parent or guardian. Pouring and sprinkling are acceptable for accomplishing the ceremony of baptism.

The Second View: Baptism should be by immersion because of its symbolic meaning of dying to self and being raised to newness of life in Christ. Before a person can be baptized, he should learn about Jesus and what He has done for him, make a personal choice to accept Jesus as his Saviour, and repent of sins.

Baptism by immersion, repentance necessary, learn about Jesus, believe in Jesus, make personal choice

↑

1. **Mt.3:16** "And Jesus, when he was baptized, **went up straightway out of the water**: and, lo, the heavens were opened..."

↑

2. **Mt. 28:19-20** "Go ye therefore and **teach** all nations, baptizing them in the name of the Father, and of the Son, and of the Holy Ghost: **teaching them to observe all things** whatsoever I have commanded you..."

↑

3. **Mk. 1:4** "John did baptize in the wilderness, and preach the baptism of **repentance**..."

↑

4. **Mk. 1:10** "And straightway **coming up out of the water**, he saw the heavens opened..."

↑

5. **Mk. 16:16** "He that believeth and is baptized shall be saved; but he that believeth not shall be damned."

Sprinkling and pouring, no repentance necessary, no learning about Jesus, no believing in Jesus, no personal choice

Baptism by immersion, repentance necessary, learn about Jesus, believe in Jesus, make personal choice

↑

6. **Lk. 3:3** "And he [John] came into all the country about Jordon, preaching the baptism of **repentance** for the remission of sins."

↑

7. **Jn. 3:23** "And John also was baptizing in Aenon near to Salim, **because there was much water there**..."

↑

8. **Acts 2:38** "Then Peter said... Repent, and be baptized every one of you..."

↑

9. **Acts 8:13** "Then Simon himself **believed** also: and when he was baptized..."

↑

10. **Acts 8:37-39** "...if thou **believest** with all thine heart...and they **went down both into the water**, both Phillip and the eunuch; and he baptized him..."

Sprinkling and pouring, no repentance necessary, no learning about Jesus, no believing in Jesus, no personal choice

Baptism by immersion, repentance necessary, learn about Jesus, believe in Jesus, make personal choice

↑

(11.) **Acts 13:24** "When John had first preached before his coming the baptism of **repentance** to all the people of Israel."

↑

(12.) **Acts 16:30-33** "...**Believe** on the Lord Jesus Christ, and thou shalt be saved...and was baptized..."

↑

(13.) **Acts 19:4** " ...John verily baptized with the baptism of **repentance**..."

↑

(14.) **Acts 22:16** "And now why tarriest thou? arise, and be baptized, and **wash away thy sins**..."

↑

(15.) **Rom. 6:3-4** "...baptized into his **death**? Therefore we are **buried** with him by baptism into death: that like as Christ was **raised up** from the dead by the glory of the Father, even so we also should walk in newness of life."

Sprinkling and pouring, no repentance necessary, no learning about Jesus, no believing in Jesus, no personal choice

Baptism by immersion, repentance necessary, learn about Jesus, believe in Jesus, make personal choice

↑

16. **Col. 2:12 "Buried with him** in baptism, wherein also ye are **risen with *him*** through the faith of the operation of God, who hath raised him from the dead."

Sprinkling and pouring, no repentance necessary, no learning about Jesus, no believing in Jesus, no personal choice

You will notice two things about the list above. First, all the texts give support to **one view**. Second, all the texts come from the N.T. because the symbolism of baptism has its basis in the death, burial, and resurrection of Christ. This is why all the references are from the N.T.. Baptism was a N.T. rite.

Our conclusions are easily drawn in this study as there are no texts that support the practice of infant baptism. If you look up the word "sprinkle" in the concordance, you will find only a few texts listed that refer to the Levitical rites of cleansing for the priesthood. The priest had to sprinkle water on himself in a ceremony to make himself clean and set aside for service. This rite is also mentioned referring to Christ as our High Priest, telling how He cleanses us with the sprinkling of His blood (Heb. 10:22).

Ask Yourself

1. Can an infant repent of sin, or believe on the Lord Jesus, or understand the teachings of Jesus before baptism?

2. Can an infant choose to be baptized when he is not yet old enough to talk?

3. Have I been immersed (baptized) if I have only been poured over or sprinkled?

4. Was my immersion a symbol of the choice **I made** to follow Jesus?

Saturday or Sunday?

As I have stated before, I have purposely picked controversial subjects so that when the texts are compared and analyzed, we can gain some valuable insights. Those insights are the following:

1. **Find Truth:** In a world where everyone says, "This is truth," or "That is truth," it is good to study for yourself and be able to find truth.

2. **Understand Where False Ideas Originate:** By using the ABC method of study, you can learn **why** there are various teachings on the same subject, even though support for both ideas (or doctrines) comes from the same source, the Bible.

It is not difficult to understand where false ideas come from when all the texts on any given subject are lined up. If some sect fails to examine all the texts in the Bible that relate to a given doctrine, it may base its belief on the few verses which **appear to be** out of line with the Big Picture, and the **"A"** that assumes God does not lie. Even so, by checking the context of the verses out of line, they would arrive at a different teaching, **truth**.

This subject of Saturday or Sunday as the holy day has been called "religion's greatest question" by some weekly news magazines. I hope that through the application of the ABC method of Bible study we may be able to arrive at truth that is too plain to deny.

In the study of this subject we will seek to answer the question, "Which day should we keep holy today?" There are two basic views in Christianity today and they are as follows.

One: Those who worship on Sunday say that this is the right day for Christians to worship upon, and they give the following reasons.

1. It is Biblical.
2. It is the Lord's day.
3. The N.T. Christians worshipped on Sunday.
4. Sunday-keeping honors the resurrection of Jesus.
5. Saturday-keeping is for Jews and Sunday-keeping is for Christians.

Two: On the other hand, there are those who claim that Christians should still be keeping the Sabbath (Saturday) as the day of worship and they list the following reasons.

1. It is Biblical.
2. Sabbath-keeping (or keeping Saturday holy) is for everyone and not just the Jews.
3. The N.T. Church kept the Sabbath (Saturday).
4. Sabbath-keeping (Saturday) is part of the Ten Commandments, which are still valid guides to help us know right from wrong.

Which view is correct? Which view is erroneous? Obviously both cannot be correct. The "A" in our ABC's is "Assume that God does not lie and contradict Himself." Saturday worship can't be right and **true** if Sunday is the right day, and vice versa. Let us begin by recognizing some **points accepted by both sides.**

1. Jews in the O.T. kept Saturday as their day to go to church (synagogue) and worship.

2. The Jews still keep Saturday as their Sabbath.

3. One of the Ten Commandments (the 4th) does speak about setting aside a day of worship to God (Ex. 20:8-11).

What about us as N.T. Christians? Should we still be keeping Saturday as our day of church attendance and worship? Some say, "Yes!" Some say, "No!" **What does the Bible say?**

Because of the complex nature of this study, we will divide our subject into smaller studies. When we are finished with all of our smaller studies, then we will tabulate the results to get the answer to our main question, "Which day should we keep holy today?" Here is a brief outline of the studies.

Study #1 First-Day Texts (Sunday)

Study #2 The Lord's Day, is it Saturday or Sunday?

Study #3 The Resurrection Memorial

Study #4 Does God's Law Change?

Study #5 The New Testament Day of Worship.

Study #6 Is Sabbath-keeping Jewish?

Study #7 Which Day is the Sabbath Today? Can We Tell?

Summary of All the Studies

Study #1 First-Day Texts

Is worshipping on Sunday Biblical? Are there texts in the Bible that tell us to worship on Sunday? If we line up all of the texts in the Bible that refer to the first day of the week (or Sunday), it will be easy to tell if there is Biblical support. The texts that refer to Sunday **are not overwhelming** in the Bible, as some might assume, for there are only nine in the entire Bible that refer to the first day of the week (or Sunday).

We will have two categories dividing the texts in our first study. The **first** category will be the texts that are **mere historical references** to an event that happened on Sunday (the resurrection). The **second** category will be the texts that point toward **worshipping on Sunday**. Any text, referring to Sunday, that says the N.T. Church worshipped on Sunday will point toward the category of worship on Sunday.

Let us look at the texts and see what we find for Biblical examples.

Mere historical reference

1. **Gen. 1:5** The first day of Creation Week.
2. **Mt. 28:1** Resurrection of Jesus on Sunday. Mary Magdalene found the tomb empty.
3. **Mk. 16:2** Ladies find the empty tomb on resurrection Sunday.
4. **Mk. 16:9** Jesus appears to Mary on Sunday morning of the resurrection.
5. **Lk. 24:1** Jesus' followers find an empty tomb on resurrection Sunday.
6. **Jn. 20:1** Mary comes to the empty tomb on resurrection Sunday.

Worshipping on Sunday

7. **Jn. 20:19** The disciples are gathered together on the first day of the week, and Jesus appears to them.

Mere historical reference

Worshipping on Sunday

(8.) **Acts 20:7** Paul and his companions meet on the first day of the week.

(9.) **1 Cor. 16:2** "Upon the first *day* of the week let every one of you lay by him in store, as *God* hath prospered him, that there be no gatherings when I come."

Notice that out of the nine times that the first day (Sunday) is mentioned **in the entire Bible,** that there are three references that seem to be pointing towards Sunday worship. Look closely at their context.

TEXT #7 **Jn. 20:19** "Then the same day at evening, being the first *day* of the week, when the doors were shut where the disciples were assembled for fear of the Jews, came Jesus and stood in the midst, and saith unto them, Peace *be* unto you."

Many would claim that this text supports the idea that the disciples were meeting on Sunday in honor of the resurrection, but **notice three things** from the context.

1. The text clearly states **why** the disciples were meeting: "For fear of the Jews."

2. How could the disciples be meeting in honor of the resurrection, when not all of them even believed that it had taken place. See vs. 24-25 which tell of Thomas not being there when Jesus appeared, and saying, "...I will not believe."

3. A quick comparison of Jesus' words in Jn. 20:19 and Lk. 24:36 makes it clear that both texts are speaking of the same gathering. Luke's version explains how the disciples **were surprised** and had trouble believing, even when they saw Jesus for themselves. (Compare also Mk. 16:14.) **How** could the disciples be meeting **in honor of** the resurrection **when they did not believe** that Jesus was resurrected yet?

From the evidence listed above we can see that this text **is not giving us an example** of Sunday worship by the disciples, but a mere historical reference to their gathering "for fear of the Jews."

TEXT #8 **Acts 20:7** "And upon the first *day* of the week, when the disciples came together to break bread, Paul preached to them, ready to depart on the morrow; and continued his speech until midnight."

From a casual reading of this text we might conclude that the disciples were meeting and worshipping on Sunday. If this is true, then it would definitely give us an example of Christians worshipping on Sunday in the New Testament. **But**, a casual reading **will not do** when we are searching hard and **truth** is the prize.

The time setting of this passage is most important. The Bible clearly states that it was Sunday or the first day of the week. It was the dark part of Sunday, as there were lights in the upper chamber (vs. 8) and Paul preached on until midnight (vs. 7). Which midnight?

The midnight spoken of in this text **is Saturday night**. Bible writers counted time differently from the way we do today. We count the days from midnight to midnight, but the Bible writers counted time from sunset to sunset, as the Jewish people still do. Also in the Biblical context, the dark part of the day comes first and then the light part of the day (Gen 1:5, 8, 13, 19, 23, 31). If this idea is still confusing let me give you two examples that will help.

a. The Jewish people understood God's way of keeping time and use it to this day as they celebrate the Sabbath (Saturday). The Sabbath starts from the time the sun goes down on Friday night, and does not end until the sun goes down on Saturday night. Hence a twenty-four-hour period of time (one day) is counted from sunset to sunset, instead of from midnight to midnight. The first part of the Sabbath or Saturday is what we call Friday evening.

b. The NEB translates Acts 20:7 and applies this recognized and well-known principle. Note the translation:

   "**On Saturday night**, in our assembly for the breaking of bread, Paul, who was to leave the next day, addressed them, and went on speaking until midnight."

Why is this point so important? Because this text is used to give support to Sunday worship, as though Paul had a special regard for Sunday and kept it holy. **This**

is not so. Notice what Paul does the next morning, **on Sunday morning** (the light part of the first day). Verse 6 tells us that Paul was in the city of Troas, and vs. 13 says that Paul's companions sailed ahead to Assos. They were going to pick Paul up the next day because he wanted to go by foot. Verse 7 and vs. 11 both tell us that Paul did just that. The next day, **Sunday morning,** Paul walked the distance from Troas to Assos (about twenty miles). Note the diagram below to illustrate where Paul was in Troas and where he walked, to Assos.

Paul's companions sailed around the peninsula on Saturday night while Paul preached.

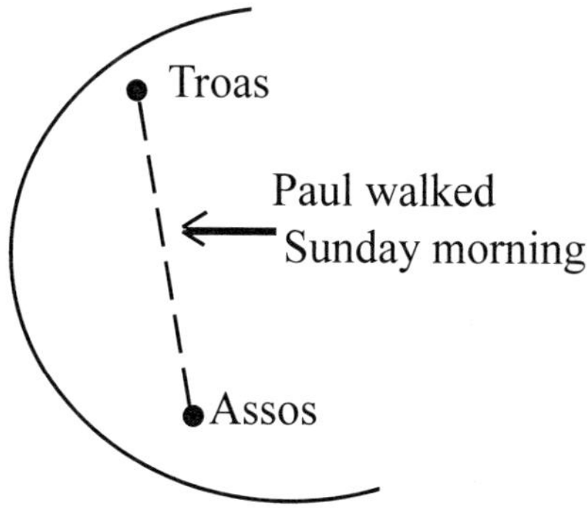

To say that Paul was **keeping Sunday holy or advocating keeping it holy,** from this text, would be to take the verse out of context. Paul was probably conducting a farewell meeting. After preaching all night long, he walked the twenty-mile trip from Troas to Assos so that he could meet his friends who had left the night before.

Some say that because they broke bread (vs. 7) together on Sunday, that makes Sunday holy. Acts 2:46 says that the disciples of Jesus broke bread every day (daily). Breaking bread on any certain day does not make that day holy, whether it is Tuesday or Sunday.

This verse in context does **not** give us a direct command to keep Sunday holy or even an indirect hint at

Sunday-keeping. This verse fits in with other verses as a mere historical event that took place on Sunday.

TEXT #9 **1 Cor. 16:2** "Upon the first *day* of the week let every one of you lay **by him** in store, as *God* hath prospered him, that there be no gatherings when I come."

This text, at first glance, would appear to be saying that the N.T. Church was meeting together on Sunday and passing the offering plate for a special famine relief offering. **A closer look at the context proves just the opposite.**

The church members were admonished by Paul to set aside a collection for the famine-stricken church at Jerusalem, but **they were not meeting on Sunday** to pass the plate.

Notice the words "**by him**" in our verse. Those words, in the original Greek, mean "by himself" or "at home." Paul was admonishing the Corinthian believers to do their bookkeeping each week on Sunday, in a systematic way, to see how much they could set aside for the famine-stricken church in Jerusalem.

There is nothing in the text to indicate that Sunday was a meeting day, or that it was holy in any way. The Spanish version of this verse translated into English says, "Let every one of you lay in store **at home**,..."

After studying each of these texts carefully in their context, we can come to the following conclusions.

a. There is **no direct command** from anyone, Jesus or His disciples, to keep Sunday holy, or to go to church on that day.

b. In the entire Bible, every text that even mentions Sunday (or the first day of the week) is a mere historical reference to Sunday, or to an event that happened to fall on that day. **The Sunday texts give no examples of Sunday worship in the N.T. Church.**

The three texts (#7, 8, and 9), are the ones that are most often quoted by Sunday-keeping advocates. After careful study we can clearly see that Sunday worship does not have its origin in the Bible by direct command from Christ, from His followers, or from indirect inference from the three texts covered in our study.

In diagramming these Sunday texts, we draw our final diagram to look like this:

Christ gave no command to keep Sunday, disciples gave no command for Sunday, mere historical references to Sunday, no proof for Sunday worship in the N.T.

Keeping Sunday Holy; many N.T. examples; A command from Christ; A command from his disciples; based on the Bible.

1. Gen. 1:5
2. Mt. 28:1
3. Mk. 16:2
4. Mk. 16:9
5. Lk. 24:1
6. Jn. 20:1
7. Jn. 20:19
8. Acts 20:7
9. 1 Cor. 16:2

If this last study leaves you baffled, then **note the unity and agreement** of Catholic and Protestant scholars, and historians on this subject. These following quotes may answer some of the questions that arise in this area.

Historian

August Neander, celebrated historian: "The festival of Sunday, like all other festivals, was always only a human ordinance, and it was far from the intentions of the apostles to establish a Divine command in this respect, far from them, and from the early apostolic Church, to transfer the laws of the Sabbath to Sunday" (*The History of the Christian Religion and Church*, Rose's translation, p. 186).

Anglican

"And where in the Scriptures that we are told to keep the first day at all? We are commanded to keep the seventh; but we are nowhere commanded to keep the first day...The reasons why we keep the first day of the week holy instead of the seventh is for the same reason that we observe many other things, not because the Bible, but because the church, has enjoined it" (Isaac Williams, *Plain Sermons on the Cathechism*, Vol. 1, pp. 334, 336.).

Baptist

Dr. Edward F. Hiscox, author of the *Baptist Manual:* "There was and is a commandment to keep holy the Sabbath day, but that Sabbath day was not Sunday. It will be said, however, with some show of triumph, that the Sabbath was transferred from the seventh to the first day of the week.... Where can the record of such a transaction be found? Not in the N.T., absolutely not." (This is from a paper read before a New York Ministers' Conference held on Nov. 13, 1893.)

Catholics Say There is No Proof

"Cardinal Gibbons declared: "You may read the Bible from Genesis to Revelation, and you will not find a single line authorizing the sanctification of Sunday. The Scriptures enforce the religious observance of Saturday." (*The Faith of Our Fathers,* 1910 ed., p. 89.)

Protestants Say There Is No Proof

"The notion of a formal substitution (of the first for the seventh day),...and the transference to it, perhaps in a spiritualized form, of the Sabbatical obligation established by...the fourth commandment, **has no basis whatever** either in Holy Scripture or in Christian antiquity" (*Dictionary of Christian Antiquities*, Article, "Sabbath," Smith and Cheatham).

Congregationalist

"It is quite clear that however rigidly or devoutly we spend Sunday, we are not keeping the Sabbath....The sabbath was founded on a specific divine command. We can plead no such command for the obligation to observe Sunday... There is not a single sentence in the N.T. to suggest that we incur any penalty by violating the supposed sanctity of Sunday." (Dr. R. W. Dale in *The Ten Commandments,* pages 100-101.)

If you have further questions on **the change** from Saturday to Sunday and **how** it came about, see the Appendix for a brief explanation and further details (p. 203).

When we diagram what historians and scholars said about Saturday and Sunday, we find their results match what we have already discovered from our first study.

Christ gave no command to keep Sunday. Disciples gave no command for Sunday; mere historical references to Sunday, no proof for Sunday worship in the N.T.

Keeping Sunday Holy; many N.T. examples; A command from Christ; A command from the disciples, based on the Bible.

1. Historians
2. Anglican Scholar
3. Baptist Scholar
4. Catholic Scholar
5. Protestant Scholar
6. Congregationalist

Study #2 The Lord's Day: is it Saturday or Sunday?

Most Christians today consider the term, "the Lord's Day" as referring to Sunday. As far as **the popular and accepted usage** of the term in the 20th century, they are correct. But is that the Biblical meaning of the term? Just because it is common and popular **does not mean** that it is correct. **Truth** is established **by the Bible** and **not by popular vote.**

The term, "the Lord's Day," appears **only once** in the entire Bible and that is in Rev. 1:10. Let's look at the context carefully as you read the statement.

> "I was in the Spirit on the Lord's day and heard behind me a great voice, as of a trumpet,"

There is **nothing** in this verse that would tell us if the Lord's Day is Saturday or Sunday. As you study the verse there are three observations that can be made.

1. John is speaking about himself.

2. The Lord that he speaks of is Jesus.

3. The Lord (Jesus) has a day that He calls His own.

The context around the verse **does not tell us** which day John is speaking of, Saturday or Sunday. If we interpret this in light of 20th century thought, then we would be quick to say that John is talking about Sunday. But if we search through the Bible to find out **if** the Lord Jesus has a day that He calls His own, then we come up with a different conclusion. Listed below are the **only** two places in the N.T. where the Lord Jesus singles out a day and calls it His own.

1. **Mt. 12:8** "For the son of man is Lord even of the sabbath day."

2. **Mk. 2:27-28** "And he said unto them, The sabbath was made for man, and not man for the sabbath: Therefore the Son of man is Lord also of the sabbath."

These two N.T. verses tell us that the Sabbath (Saturday) is the Lord's Day of the Bible. Notice that this is also true in the O.T. verses below.

1. Christ not only gave the Ten Commandments, but is also the Creator of the Sabbath. (See ch. 2, p. 16-17 and compare Neh. 9:6-15 with 1 Cor 10:4, and James 4:12 with Acts 4:12.)

2. **Isa. 58:13** God calls the Sabbath "**my holy day.**"

3. **Ex. 20:8-11** "Remember the Sabbath day, to keep it holy....*in* six days the **Lord made** heaven and earth, the sea, and all that in them *is*, and rested the seventh day: wherefore the LORD blessed the sabbath day, and hallowed it."

It is the same day in the New and Old Testament that the Lord calls His own. According to the Big Picture, **Saturday** and **not** Sunday, is what the Bible refers to as "the Lord's Day." Diagramed, it looks like this:

Saturday is the Lord's Day

1. Ex. 20:8-11
2. Isa. 58:13
3. Mt. 12:8
4. Mk. 2:27, 28
5. Rev. 1:10

~~**Sunday is the Lord's Day**~~

In verse #4 above, Jesus states, "The Sabbath (Saturday) was made for **man....**" The Greek word for "man" is the generic term meaning "mankind." Jesus is here telling His followers that **the Sabbath was made for all mankind.** Some say that the Sabbath was for the Jews only, but the words of Jesus, in this verse, do not back up that idea.

Notice also that **the Sabbath had its origin at the creation of the world** (Gen. 2:1-3) and not just when the Ten Commandments were handed down from God at Mt. Sinai. The idea of Sabbath-keeping (Saturday) being Jewish and Sunday being Christian may be popular, but **it is not Biblical**!

Study #3 The Resurrection Memorial

Does the popularity of a concept determine the rightness of it? **If** that were true, then the people that nailed Jesus to the cross must have been right and following truth because they were in the majority. It was popular, at that moment, to cry, "Crucify Him, crucify Him!" Did the popularity of that idea make it right? No! No! **A thousand times no**! So it is with worshipping on Sunday. Our only question regarding the resurrection memorial should be, "What does the Bible say about worshipping on Sunday as a memorial of the resurrection?"

The N.T. does say that there is a memorial of the resurrection, but it is not going to church on Sunday! Baptism is a memorial of the death, burial, and **resurrection** of Christ (see chapter on baptism).

If a person wants to find truth on this particular question, he does not have to look far. As we have discovered from studies #1 and 2, there is not even one verse in the Bible that directly or indirectly says Sunday should be kept holy, as a memorial of the resurrection.

Actually, if we were looking for a verse, to point to a certain day of the week, that would honor the resurrection, then we would have to look at the Sabbath (Saturday). The Sabbath is a sign of two things.

1. God (Jesus) is the **creator** (Ex. 20:11).

2. God (Jesus) is the One who sanctifies or recreates us (Ex. 31:13, Ex. 20:20). If we want to keep a day holy in honor of Christ's victory over sin, death, and the grave, then we are told plainly that is the Sabbath. It represents all of that (Heb. 4:4-11).

This text even goes as far as to say that keeping the Sabbath holy is a sign that you have quit trying to work your way to Heaven and that you are resting from your own works, just as God rested from His work on the first Sabbath (Heb. 4:9-10).

Study #4 Does God's Law Change?

Many have said, "We are under grace now and not under the law; so we do not have to keep the commandments or the Sabbath which is a part of the commandments." It is this kind of statement that starts people arguing over law and grace. Let us look at some of the overall implications of both views and apply our ABC principle to an age-old argument to see if any light can be gained through this method.

I would be the first to say, and state in writing, that I believe **salvation comes by faith and not by works**! The Bible is too plain to make a mistake on this point. No one will get into Heaven because he has been good enough, or because he has done enough penitence, or meritorious works. "For by grace are you saved through faith; and that not of yourselves: *it is* the gift of God: not of works, lest any man should boast" (Eph. 2:8-9). We will keep this **fact** in mind all through our discussion of this subject. Whether a person keeps the Sabbath or Sunday, whether or not a person steals, commits adultery, murders or does not murder, **salvation comes as a free gift from God and cannot be earned or merited**!

Let us look at some of the implications of the view that grace has done away with the law.

If the law is done away with, then:

1. Is it OK to steal (8th commandment: Ex. 20:15).

2. Is it OK to murder (6th commandment: Ex. 20:13).

3. Is it OK to bow down to idols now (2nd commandment: Ex. 20:4-5).

Most churches would agree that nine out of ten of the commandments are binding and valid today; **but** they say, grace does away with the fourth commandment (Saturday as a holy day). Is that consistent thinking?

Ask Yourself

1. Will it ever be right to steal? In the 1980's? In the 1990's? In Heaven?

2. Will it ever be right to murder? In the 1980's? In the 1990's? In Heaven?
3. Will it be right if we all decide to start committing adultery with each other's spouses? In the 1980's? In the 1990's? **Ever**?

Is it right to break any of the commandments? Are they still binding and valid as moral precepts? If the answer is "Yes," then the Sabbath commandment is still valid too! Then God still means what He says when He specifies Saturday to be our day of worship, a day to refrain from secular labor. James 2:10 does say that whoever offends in one point (or commandment) is guilty of breaking all of them.

I do not believe that there is a Christian denomination in existence today that teaches its members that stealing or murdering is right. Yet the Sabbath commandment was written by the same finger (God's) and is a part of the ten. Almost all churches and theologians choose to set it aside and say it does not really matter whether you keep the Sabbath (Saturday) or Sunday. Does that kind of thinking sound consistent to you?

If the commandments are set aside by grace, then all ten are set aside; and it is all right to murder, steal, commit adultery, and break the Sabbath. But if the commandments are not set aside by grace and are still binding, then all of the commandments are still binding, including the commandment to keep holy the seventh day or Saturday. Let us be consistent!

In our studies, **when we are misunderstanding** God's Word, inconsistencies seem to pop up. They indicate that there is falsehood in our teachings or beliefs. Is that possible with the Sabbath question?

We have looked at some of the implications of believing one way over the other. Now, let us look at the texts that will speak directly to the issue of this study, "Does God's Law Change?"

God's law and word are unchangeable

1. **Numb. 23:19** "God *is* not a man, that he should lie; neither the son of man, that he should repent: hath he said, and shall he not do *it*? or hath he spoken, and shall he not make it good?"

2. **Psm. 89:34** "My covenant will I not break, nor alter the thing that is gone out of my lips."

God's law and word do change.

3. **Psm. 102:27** Speaking of God, David said, "But thou *art* the same, and thy years shall have no end."

4. **Psm. 111:7-8** "The works of his hands *are* verity and judgment; all his commandments *are* sure. They stand fast for ever and ever, *and are* done in truth and uprightness."

5. **Psm. 119:89** "For ever, O LORD, thy word is settled in heaven."

6. **Isa. 40:8** "The grass withereth, the flower fadeth: but the Word of our God shall stand forever."

God's law and word are unchangeable

7. **Is. 51:6** "...for the heavens shall vanish away like smoke, and the earth shall wax old like a garment, and they that dwell therein shall die in like manner: but my salvation shall be for ever, and my righteousness shall not be abolished."

8. **Mal. 3:6** "For I *am* the LORD, I change not..."

God's law and word do change.

9. **Mt. 5:17-18** "...I am not come to destroy, but to fulfill....Till heaven and earth pass, one jot or one tittle shall in no wise pass from the law, till all be fulfilled."

10. **Lk. 16:17** "And it is easier for heaven and earth to pass, than one tittle of the law to fail."

11. **Jn. 12:34** "...Christ abideth for ever..."

12. **Rom. 3:31** "Do we then make void the law through faith? God forbid: yea, we establish the law."

God's law and word are unchangeable

13. **Rom. 6:14** "For sin shall not have dominion over you: for ye are not under the law, but under grace."

14. **Rom. 7:12** "Wherefore the law *is* holy, and the commandment holy, and just, and good."

15. **Rom. 8:2** "For the law of the Spirit of life in Christ Jesus hath made me free from the law of sin and death."

God's law and word do change.

16. **Rom. 10:4** "For Christ *is* the end of the law for righteousness to every one that believeth."

17. **Rom. 11:29** "For the gifts and calling of God *are* without repentance."

18. **1 Cor. 7:19** "Circumcision is nothing, and uncircumcision is nothing, but the keeping of the commandments of God."

19. **Gal. 3:24-25** "Wherefore the law was our schoolmaster....But after that faith is come, we are no longer under a schoolmaster."

God's law and word are unchangeable

God's law and word do change.

← 20. **Gal. 5:18** "But if ye be led of the Spirit, ye are not under the law."

← 21. **Eph. 2:15** "Having abolished in his flesh the enmity, *even* the law of commandments *contained* in ordinances..."

← 22. **Col. 2:14-17** "Blotting out the handwriting of ordinances that was against us, which was contrary to us, and took it out of the way, nailing it to his cross...Let no man...judge you...in respect of an holyday...or of the sabbath *days:*"

↑ 23. **2 Tim. 2:13** "...he cannot deny Himself."

↑ 24. **Titus 1:2** "...God, that cannot lie."

↑ 25. **Heb. 6:18** "... impossible for God to lie..."

↑ 26. **Heb. 13:8** "Jesus Christ the same yesterday, and to day, and for ever."

God's law and word are unchangeable

27. **James 1:17** "...the Father...with whom is no variableness, neither shadow of turning."

28. **1 Pet. 1:25** "But the word of the Lord endureth forever..."

God's law and word do change.

29. **1 Jn. 2:3-5** "And hereby we do know that we know him, if we keep his commandments. He that saith I know him, and keepeth not his commandments, is a liar, and the truth is not in him..."

30. **2 Jn. 5-6** "...not as though I wrote a new commandment unto thee, but that which we had from the beginning, that we love one another. And this is love, that we walk after his commandments..."

We must keep in mind what we are looking for in Study #4. We are not trying to settle on two or three pages the argument of law and grace that theologians have been working on for centuries. I believe that everyone is **saved by faith and not works**!

Is it valid to say that the law is null and void, so that we can keep Sunday in place of the Sabbath that is specified in the fourth commandment? That is what we are trying to focus upon. If we discover that the law is done away with, then does that mean that it is all right to steal, commit adultery, murder, etc.? Let us be consistent.

Most people will agree that we are under grace and not under the law. Many disagree as to what that means. In practical terms, they are saying the following:

> Out of the Ten Commandments, nine are still valid statements of right and wrong, acceptable and unacceptable behavior, but the fourth commandment that requires worshipping on Saturday has been done away with because we are under grace.

If we were to summarize the texts that we have lined up it would look like this:

God's law and word are unchangeable		**God's law and word do change.**
#1	#14 *	#13 *
#2	#17 *	#15 *
#3	#18 *	#16 *
#4	#23 *	#19 *
#5	#24 *	#20 *
#6	#25 *	#21 *
#7	#26 *	#22 *
#8	#27	*Total Support = 7 Texts*
#9	#28	
#10	#29	
#11	#30	* *Statements of Paul the Apostle*
#12*		
Total Support = 23 Texts		

The argument (or discussion) over law and grace is not new, but has raged on for many centuries. The reason for its intensity and longevity is because statements on both sides are so strong. The support for what appears to be in the minority is stronger than in most other studies. Notice that all of the controversial statements come from the hand of Paul. All Old and N.T. sources including Jesus are in total agreement with the exception of Paul.

Let us carefully analyze the implications of both sides so that we may be able to recognize truth when we see it. The key to this subject, we will find, is the same that we have found in other subjects; that is, God does not lie or contradict Himself.

If Paul is saying in any of the texts (#13, 15, 16, 19, 20, 21, 22) that the law (or the Ten Commandments) has been abolished by grace or the Holy Spirit, **then** the following implications would also be true:

1. There is no standard of right and wrong. A Christian who has faith can do anything because he is free from the law. Stealing, murdering, lying, Sabbath-breaking, and worshipping idols are all right with God now, as long as a person has **faith**, because we are under grace.

2. The Holy Spirit sets us free from the requirements of God's law; so we are free to kill, steal, lie, or break the Sabbath, just as long as we are led by the Spirit. His Spirit may disagree with what the written Word says; so following the Spirit determines Truth, and not the Bible. Does this sound right? Can this possibly be true? Some teach this **as if** it were **truth**.

3. God's standards have changed, therefore God has changed. This would make God very unreliable.

4. Paul is disagreeing with his own statements (TEXTS #12, 14, 17, 18, 23, 24, 25, 26), and therefore we must be misunderstanding these texts, **or** Paul is lying and **practicing** his new belief, that everything is acceptable and all right now in God's sight. Paul does state, "Where no law is, *there is* no transgression" (Rom. 4:15). Can this be true?

5. Paul is contradicting the Big Picture and therefore disagreeing with Jesus, Moses, David, Isaiah, Malachi, Matthew, Luke, James, Peter, and John (TEXTS # 1, 2, 3, 4, 5, 6, 7, 8, 9, 10, 11, 27, 28, 29, 30).

6. **One of the following three things must be wrong:**

   a. Our original assumption about God not contradicting Himself

   b. Our understanding of TEXTS #1, 2, 3, 4, 5, 6, 7, 8, 9, 10, 11, 12, 14, 17, 18, 23 24, 25, 26, 27, 28, 29, 30

   c. Our understanding of Paul's statements about the law abolished by grace (TEXTS #13, 15, 16, 19, 20, 21, 22)

Remember through this study that we are trying to discover whether or not part of God's law can be changed or modified (the fourth commandment from Saturday to Sunday).

The alternative to the above view, is that Paul **is** saying grace does **not** abolish the law, but abolishes the misuse of law, as a means of salvation. Therefore, the following would then be true:

1. The Ten Commandments are still valid, moral precepts of what sin is and what it is not. It is still wrong to lie, steal, murder, break the Sabbath, worship idols, etc.

2. Paul is **not** disagreeing with his own statements (TEXTS #12, 14, 17, 18, 23, 24, 25, 26), but we must be misunderstanding his statements about the law being abolished.

3. Paul is in agreement with Jesus, Moses, David, Isaiah, Malachi, Matthew, Luke, James, Peter, and John (TEXTS #1, 2, 3, 4, 5, ,6, 7, 8, 9, 10, 11, 27, 28, 29, 30).

4. God and His standards have remained **unchanged**.

Some would say that **if** we interpret Paul to say that the law is still binding, then we **must** be saying that you work your way to Heaven by works and not by faith.

I would have to ask the following question. According to Paul, **is it possible** to believe the law is still binding **and** believe in salvation by faith at the same time? Or asked another way, does believing in the unchangeableness of God's law mean that you **must** believe in salvation by works?

Some would lead you to think that it is impossible to believe in **both** God's law as still binding **and** salvation by faith. **Hogwash**!

In order to show that **you can believe** in salvation by faith **and** the law as still being valid, we would have to find the following in the writings of Paul:

1. **Statements that the law is good.** If Paul is suggesting that the law is abolished, then it is logical to assume that he would also say the law **needs** to be done away with because it is bad. If he says that the law is good, then he **must** be saying it is still in force **to tell us right from wrong**.

2. **Statements that describe sin as the breaking of commandments.** Paul could not say that sin is breaking the commandments or wrong **if** he says that the commandments have been abolished. If Paul is suggesting in any of his statements that the law is now done away with, then there is no longer any sinful or wrong behavior, because the standard whereby sin is established is now gone ("...sin is the transgression of the law." 1 Jn. 3:4).

3. **Statements in which Paul says that the law is not made void through faith. If** Paul says **faith** does not make the law void, then you can believe in **both** the unchangeableness of the law **and** salvation by **faith**. Then Paul would be condemning good works that are done for the wrong reasons and **not** just good works and obedience. The two ideas **must not** be contradictory to Paul **if he says both are true.** Paul is saying in TEXTS #13, 15, 16, 19, 20, 21, 22 that working your way to Heaven is wrong, but obedience to Christ, out of love, in response to what He has done, is right.

If we can locate in Paul's writings the responses that he gives to our questions, then we will understand Paul's difficult passages before we come to them.

Summary of Implications

If Paul is saying in TEXTS #13, 15, 16, 19, 20, 21, 22 that:

God's law and word are unchangeable	**God's law and word do change.**
It is logical to assume that he would say:	
1. The law is good.	1. The law is bad.
2. Sin is still wrong.	2. Sin is all right now, because the law is gone.
3. Salvation by works is wrong but you must still be obedient because faith does not make the law void.	3. Salvation by works is wrong. So you do not have to be obedient because faith made the law void.

Following are the implications and Paul's statements:

Implication #1 Is the law good or bad?

"Wherefore the law *is* holy, and the commandment holy, and just, and good" (Rom. 7:12).

"But we know that the law *is* good, if a man use it lawfully" (1 Tim. 1:8).

Implication #2 Is sin still wrong?

Rom. 1:29-32 People who are "...filled with all unrighteousness, fornication, wickedness, covetousness, maliciousness; full of envy, murder, debate, deceit...they which commit such things are worthy of death..."

Rom. 2:13 "For not the hearers of the law *are* just before God, but the doers of the law shall be justified."

Rom. 3:20 "...for by the law *is* the knowledge of sin."

Rom. 6:12-15 "Let not sin therefore reign in your mortal body, that ye should obey it in the lusts thereof. Neither yield ye your members *as* instruments of unrighteousness unto sin:... For sin shall not have dominion over you: for ye are not under the law, but under grace. What then? Shall we sin, because we are not under the law, but under grace? God forbid."

Rom. 6:18 "Being then made free from sin, ye became the servants of righteousness."

Rom. 6:23 "For the wages of sin *is* death; but the gift of God *is* eternal life through Jesus..."

Rom. 7:13 "...sin by the commandment might become exceeding sinful."

Rom. 13:9-10 Paul says that if you break the commandments and commit adultery, kill, steal, bear false witness, covet, you really don't love your neighbor.

1 Tim. 5:22 "...neither be partaker of other men's sins: keep thyself pure."

It is abundantly clear that Paul believes sin is still sin and that it is wrong! There are many other verses that we could look at here, but the ones stated above are sufficient to establish the point that Paul believes the law is still valid and binding on men's souls **as the great standard** of right and wrong.

Implication #3 Does salvation by faith mean that we do not have to be obedient?

Rom. 2:13 "(For not the hearers of the law *are* just before God, but the doers of the law shall be justified."

Rom. 3:20 "Therefore by the deeds of the law there shall no flesh be justified in his sight: for by the law *is* the knowledge of sin."

Rom. 3:31 "Do we then make void the law through faith? God forbid: yea, we establish the law."

Rom. 4:20-22 Abraham did not stagger at the impossibility of obeying God, but by faith believed and obeyed and "it was imputed to him for righteousness."

1 Cor. 7:19 "Circumcision is nothing, and uncircumcision is nothing, but the keeping of the commandments of God."

2 Cor. 10:5 "...and bringing into captivity every thought to the obedience of Christ."

Gal. 5:6 "For in Jesus Christ neither circumcision availeth any thing, nor uncircumcision; but faith which worketh by love."

It is clear, here also, that Paul believes salvation comes by faith and not by good works. At the same time, **he also believes** that you must be obedient, out of love to the Saviour.

If we interpret Paul to be saying that the law has been abolished, then he would not only be contradicting all the other Bible writers on this subject, but he would also be contradicting himself.

As we look at the context of the seven verses that are in the minority, remember that **both views cannot be right**. One must be truth and the other error.

TEXT #13 **Rom. 6:14** "For sin shall not have dominion over you: for ye are not under the law, but under grace."

The context of this verse makes it clear that Paul is saying that you cannot be saved by the works of the law. Salvation comes by grace. In the phrase, "Ye are not under **THE** law," there is a significant difference in the Greek and the way it was translated in the KJV. The word "**the**," that I have capitalized above, is not in the original Greek manuscript. A more correct translation would read "for ye are not under law, but under grace."

Paul is saying that the Christian is not under **the principle of law for salvation** because he is under grace. From the context, Paul tells us plainly that he does not believe the law is null and void by grace. In the verses immediately preceding this, Paul states that sin should not reign in your bodies (vs. 12-13). **If** Paul was saying that being under grace means the commandments are null and void, that the Ten Commandments were abolished, then why would he care if a person sinned?

In the immediate context, the verse that follows verse 14, Paul asks the question, "Shall we sin because we are not under the law, but under grace?" His answer is very clear and to the point, "God forbid." Paul is pressing home that grace is not a license to sin. **Grace** does not abolish the role of the Ten Commandments, which is to point out sin (Rom. 3:20; 7:7). Grace is provided **because** the law cannot save! All have sinned and come short of the glory of God (Rom. 3:23). Therefore, all are in need of the grace of God as a means of salvation.

According to the context of this verse, Paul is saying that he still believes in the law as being a valid means of pointing out what sin is, but it is not to be used as a means of working your way into Heaven.

TEXT #15 **Rom. 8:2** "For the law of the Spirit of life in Christ Jesus hath made me free from the law of sin and death."

Many Christians think that this verse says the Holy Spirit makes me free from the law of God; so now I can do what I want, as long as I am guided by the Spirit. Before we look at the context of this verse, let us think about what that would mean with these two assumptions in mind:

1. The Holy Spirit guided the prophets in writing the Scriptures (2 Pet. 1:20-21).

2. The Holy Spirit is God and part of the Trinity (Mt. 28:19).

Ask Yourself

Would the Holy Spirit lead a person to transgress the written word?

If receiving guidance from the Holy Spirit means that you no longer follow the written Word, then Jesus had no need to be obedient, because He received the Spirit "without measure" (Jn. 3:34). What does the Bible say about His obedience to the will and laws of His Father?

1 Pet. 2:22 He "...did no sin..."

Jn. 8:29 "...I do always those things that please him."

Apparently receiving the Holy Spirit **was not a license to sin** for Jesus, but it was an enabling factor to help Him comply and be obedient to the law of God. We find several examples of Jesus breaking the rules that the Jews made up on "how to keep the Sabbath holy," but the record is clear that He never sinned (I Pet. 2:22). Sin equals transgression of the law (1 Jn. 3:4). He asked, "Can any of you prove me guilty of sin" (Jn. 8:46)?

Let us look at the context of this verse. Paul's thoughts start in Rom. 7 where he talks about the law. Let us outline and name the three different laws that Paul mentions:

#1 God's Law: Rom. 7:7

Paul here speaks specifically about God's Ten Commandment Law as he quotes the tenth commandment. In order to distinguish between this law and the others, we will give this first law the name, "God's law."

#2 Law of sin: Rom. 7:23

We know that this law of sin (Rom. 7:23) is different from God's law (#1) because it is called "another law" (vs. 23). Twice in the same verse, Paul tells us that this law is "in my members." This law must be Paul's human nature that is bent towards doing evil ,even when Paul wants to do good.

#3 Law of the Spirit - Rom. 8:2

This is the influence of the Holy Spirit that gives us new life in Christ.

REVIEW

LAW #1 = God's Law (The Ten Commandments)

LAW #2 = Law of Sin (our sinful natures)

LAW #3 = Law of the Spirit (Holy Spirit)

Now let us look at the text again. Paul says that **Law #3** (the law of the Spirit) sets us free from which law? The law of God? No! Look again! **The Law of the Spirit** (#3) sets us free from the **Law of Sin.** (#2) In other words, Paul is saying that the Holy Spirit sets us free from our natural bent towards sin. The Holy Spirit helps us overcome our sinful natures, so that we may walk after the Spirit and not after the flesh.

Notice the context just after Rom. 8:2. Verse 4 says that this is all done (being set free) so "That the righteousness of the law must be fulfilled in us..." Notice how the Phillips version phrases this verse:

> "So that we are able to meet the Law's requirements, so long as we are living no longer by the dictates of our sinful nature, but in obedience to the promptings of the Spirit."

There can be no mistake that Paul is saying that the Holy Spirit sets us free from **sinning** and helps us to be **obedient** to the law (the Ten Commandments). Just as Jesus was guided and strengthened in the battle against sin, we too are helped and strengthened by the Spirit's influence in our lives.

Those who believe the text indicates that we are set free from the **Law of God** just haven't studied the context.

TEXT #16 **Rom. 10:4** "For Christ *is* the end of the law for righteousness to every one that believeth."

This verse has been interpreted in several ways:

1. Christ is the termination of the law. Faith in Christ does away with the law.

2. Christ is the goal or aim of the law.

3. Christ is the fulfillment of the law.

4. Christ is the termination of the law as a means of salvation.

The context suggests that Paul is contrasting God's way of righteousness (by faith) with man's (by works) and uses Israel as an example (vs. 1) of man's attempting to attain righteousness by obedience to the law. Interpretation #1 may seem like the best answer, at first glance; but when we remember Paul's other statements about faith not making void (or terminating) the law (Rom. 3:31), we know that he cannot be backing interpretation #1. Interpretations #2 and 3 are good, but #4 seems to be the best because of the context. Paul referred to the Jews trying to earn salvation by meritorious works of the law. In this context, Paul is probably saying that keeping the law as a means of salvation is over.

Any of the latter three interpretations (#2, 3, 4) would mean that Paul reflects the Big Picture here on this subject. Those who would latch onto the first interpretation of the verse would be making Paul a liar, as he has already stated that faith does not void the law.

TEXT # 19 **Gal. 3:24-25** "...the law was our schoolmaster *to bring us* unto Christ, that we might be justified by faith. But after that faith is come, we are no longer under a schoolmaster."

Paul is speaking of two specific things here:

1. The Jewish concept that you could gain life by the meticulous keeping of a set of laws, whether ceremonial or the Ten Commandment laws (righteousness by works)

2. The Jewish system of sacrifices and ordinances that pointed forward to Christ as the lamb of God (This was called their ceremonial law.)

In Gal. 2:21 and 3:21 Paul refers to the law as not being able to give life. He is condemning the Jewish concept of salvation by works. The ceremonial law and the Ten Commandment law were never intended to give life to the individual. The ceremonial laws and sacrifices were intended to point the person to Christ for salvation, but the Jews lost sight of that and began looking to the system of observing laws to find salvation (Gal. 2:21; 3:21).

When Paul speaks of the law as "our schoolmaster" to bring us to Christ, he is again referring to both concepts that are stated above. The misuse of either law as a means of salvation had come to an end. The ceremonial laws, which contain many ordinances, yearly Sabbaths, and festivals of the Jewish economy, such as the Passover, Pentecost, and others, pointed to Christ as the slain lamb and Saviour. Apparently there were some Jews who wanted all new Gentile converts to observe all these festivals, days, months, and times (Gal. 4:9-11).

In Gal. 3:25 Paul refers to faith as being in contrast to the law. Some have taken this to mean that faith has made void the law, but I think Paul has already stated that he does not believe that to be true. Rather than saying that faith has done away with the law, he is again referring to his earlier statements about the role of the law being a means of bringing us to Christ. If Paul were saying that faith abolishes the law, then sin would cease to be sinful to God. This is not the case as Paul names sins that are outlined in the Ten Commandments (Gal. 5:19-21).

TEXT #20 **Gal. 5:18** "But if ye be led of the Spirit, ye are not under the law."

Paul is saying that the Holy Spirit would not lead a person to seek salvation by works of the law. In verses 19-21 Paul condemns the works of the flesh and defines them as the breaking of God's Commandments (adultery, idolatry, envy, murder, etc.). He contrasts "works of the flesh" with being "led of the Spirit" (vs. 18) by saying that those that are following the works of the flesh "shall not inherit the kingdom of God" (Gal. 5:21). If the "works of the flesh" are breaking the commandments, as he defines it in vs. 19, and those who break the commandments will not inherit the kingdom of God (vs. 21), then there is no way that we can interpret this verse to mean that the Holy Spirit sets us free from obedience, to break the commandments and thus miss out on Heaven. That kind of interpretation would not only be contradictory to itself and the context surrounding it, but to Paul's other statements on this subject.

TEXT #21 **Eph. 2:15** "Having abolished in his flesh the enmity, *even* the law of commandments *contained* in ordinances..."

This verse has been misinterpreted as referring to the Ten Commandments, but most scholars agree that this is speaking about the ceremonial laws of the Jews, which came to an end when Jesus died on the cross. The ceremonial law is implied in the middle phrase of the verse that says, "contained in ordinances." The enmity that came to an end is clearly defined as the hatred or strife that was between the Jews and the Gentiles (vs. 14, 16). The Jews were the ones "that were nigh" (vs. 13), and the Gentiles were the ones "which were afar off" (vs. 17). Christ "hath made both one, and hath broken down the middle wall of partition..." (vs. 14).

The Jews were entrusted with the greatest light (ceremonial laws and Ten Commandment Law). They were to carry this light to all the world, but they perverted the light and made it a burden. If any new believers wanted to join the Christian Church, there were some who tried to make them keep the Jewish ceremonial laws and festivals (sacrifices, Passover, Pentecost, etc.). Paul was saying that this system of ceremonial laws and the keeping of any laws to earn salvation has been done away with, so that now both Jew and Gentile "have access" through Christ to the Father (vs. 18).

1. If Paul was saying that the Ten Commandments were abolished, **then** He would **not** say in Eph. 5:5 that coveting, idolatry, and adultery were wrong. Certainly, they could not then be wrong by the standard of the Ten Commandments. Paul is clear when he says that commandment breakers will not inherit the kingdom of God (Eph. 5:5).

2. In Eph. 2:8-10 Paul states that salvation comes by grace through faith (vs. 8-9), but in the same breath he states that we are God's workmanship, ordained to walk in **good works** (vs. 10). **If** Paul were suggesting that the Ten Commandments were abolished, then why would he care if we did good works or not? How would he even know right from wrong **if** the standard of right and wrong were abolished? Would the Spirit tell him? Paul is clearly saying that the ceremonial laws of the Jews that caused enmity between the Jews and the Gentiles was abolished at the cross. He is not contradicting himself and saying that the Ten Commandment law was abolished at the cross.

TEXT # 22 **Col. 2:14-17** "Blotting out the handwriting of ordinances that was against us, which was contrary to us, and took it out of the way, nailing it to the cross;...Let no man... judge you in meat, or in drink, or in respect of an holyday, or of the new moon, or of the sabbath *days*: Which are a shadow of things to come; but the body *is* of Christ."

Many quote this text to say that the Sabbath of the fourth commandment is null and void. But this verse can be taken two ways. If it is talking about the Ten Commandments when it says, "the handwriting of ordinances" (vs. 14), then Paul is saying it makes no difference which day you worship, whether or not you steal, kill, or commit adultery because all those things have been blotted out (vs. 14). But, if he is referring to the ceremonial laws being blotted out, then he is saying we do not **have to keep** the ceremonial laws anymore.

They included special meat and drink offerings and yearly holidays (called Sabbaths).

Most people don't even read the verse immediately following the phrase, "Let no man therefore judge you." It says, "which are a shadow of things to come..." (vs. 17). By these words, Paul qualifies all that he has said in the verse before. The Jewish ceremonial law system was just that, a shadow of things to come. It represented Christ. In all of its ceremonial requirements, it pointed forward to Christ as the lamb of God. The ceremonial laws were **not** the same as the Ten Commandments. The Ten Commandments were written by the finger of God on stone and placed **inside** the Ark of the Covenant (Deut. 9:10; 10:1-5). The ceremonial laws were written by Moses in book form and stored in **a side pocket** of the Ark (Deut. 31:24-26).

Notice some of the symbolism of the ceremonial law and how it pointed forward to Christ as a shadow of things to come.

1. Passover: It reminded the Jews of the time when God passed over the Israelites's firstborn, but smote the firstborn of the Egyptians. This festival was a symbol of their deliverance from bondage. 1 Cor. 5:7 says that "...Christ our Passover is sacrificed for us."

2. Pentecost: This festival was to thank God for the harvest and the firstfruits. Christ represents the "firstfruits of them that slept" (1 Cor. 15:20).

3. Paul states that the wrath of God "cometh on the children of disobedience" (Col. 3:6). What would anyone be disobedient to **if** the Ten Commandments

were blotted out? Disobedience means you have disobeyed something. Paul tells the Colossians not to covet, commit fornication or participate in idolatry. He would **not** tell them this if they were now free from obedience to the Law of God.

These three yearly Sabbaths and festivals were a part of the ceremonial laws written by Moses. They are the ones blotted out at the cross.

If Paul were saying the Ten Commandments and seventh-day Sabbath were blotted out at the cross, then:

1. How would Paul know right from wrong anymore?

2. Why would he tell the people at Colosse not to do wrong and break the commandments (Col. 3:5-6)?

3. Paul states that "...the wrath of God cometh on the children of disobedience"(Col. 3:6). What would anyone be disobedient to **if** the Ten Commandments were blotted out? Disobedience means you have disobeyed something. Paul tells them not to covet, commit fornication or idolatry. He would **not** tell them this if they were now free from obedience to the Law of God.

Paul was stating that we are free from the Jewish ceremonial laws which contained many meat and drink offerings, yearly festivals (called Sabbaths but different than the Sabbath of the fourth commandment), and holy days. All of these observances came to an end at the cross when the Lamb of God was slain. When Jesus died on Mt. Calvary, the temple veil separating the Holy Place from the Most Holy Place was ripped in two from top to bottom by God. This indicated that the system of ceremonies and sacrifices pointing to Christ had come to an end (Mt. 27:51).

Paul did not say the Ten Commandments were blotted out at the cross. It is still wrong to break God's holy Law, whether it be stealing, coveting, murdering, or breaking the Sabbath of the fourth commandment.

Again I would emphasize that no one earns his way to heaven by his good works. Salvation comes by faith. A friend of mine once said, "An apple tree does not produce apples **to prove** it is an apple tree, but it produces apples because **it is** an apple tree." The same logic applies to the Christian and good works or keeping the commandments. A Christian does not do good works to prove he is a Christian, but instead a Christian does good works because he **is** a Christian. Jesus said, "If ye love me, keep my commandments" (Jn. 14:15). So out of love for the Master, we keep His commandments.

Most, if not all, denominations will admit that nine of the commandments are valid and morally binding on our souls and to break them is to sin. But they will tell you breaking the Sabbath commandment is not sin.

Consider the following: God says that He remains constant, the same, unchanging, not contradicting Himself or lying. If we assume that God **has** changed His mind about the Sabbath commandment, and it does not matter anymore whether or not we keep Saturday or Sunday, it would mean that God has changed from Saturday-keeping in the O.T. to Sunday-keeping in the N.T.. Then according to Isa. 66:23, we will change back to Saturday-keeping in the earth made new. Note the diagram on the following page.

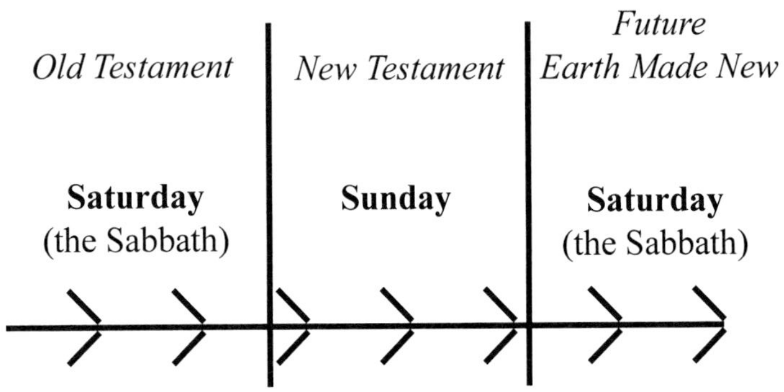

Does this illustrate that God does not change? Does it seem to convey the unchanging nature of God's law and Word? With the evidence that we have already considered about the perpetual nature of God's law and the constancy of His Word, a more correct diagram would look like this:

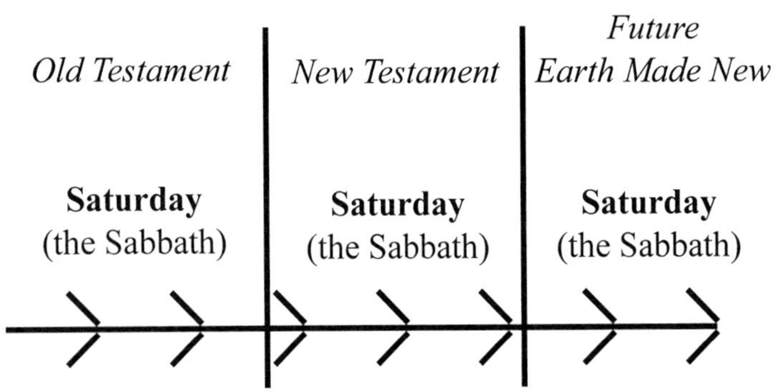

Our final diagram of Study #4 will have to be drawn in light of five different items:

1. The context surrounding the texts

2. Paul's witness that the Ten Commandments are still valid, good, and binding (TEXTS #12, 14, 17, 18, 23, 24, 25, 26)

3. Jesus' own clear statements about the perpetual nature of the commandments, "till all be fulfilled" (TEXTS #9, 10)

4. Lack of evidence in the Bible of Sunday keeping

5. The entire Big Picture with all its implications

God's law & word are unchangeable. The Sabbath is still valid. All 10 commandments are still valid and binding.

1. Numb. 23:19
2. Psm. 89:34
3. Psm. 102:27
4. Psm. 111:7-8
5. Psm. 119:89
6. Isa. 40:8
7. Isa. 51:6
8. Mal. 3:6
9. Mt. 5:17-18
10. Lk. 16:17
11. Jn. 12:34
12. Rom. 3:31
13. Rom. 6:14
14. Rom. 7:12
15. Rom. 8:2
16. Rom. 10:4
17. Rom. 11:29
18. 1 Cor. 7:19
19. Gal. 3:24-25
20. Gal. 5:18
21. Eph. 2:15
22. Col. 2:14-17
23. 1 Tim. 2:13
24. Titus 1:2
25. Heb. 6:18
26. Heb. 13:8
27. James 1:17
28. 1 Pet. 1:25
29. 1 Jn. 2:3-5
30. 2 Jn. 5-6

~~**God's law and word do change, nine commandments are still valid and binding on mankind**~~

Study #5 The New Testament Day of Worship

Some of our studies may overlap. Hopefully, with each study, we will advance further and further towards **truth**. We have already established that there is no example in the Bible of N.T. Christians worshipping on Sunday (Study #1).

Are there examples of the worship habits of the N.T. Church? Other texts besides the "first day" texts? Yes! Paul makes statements and gives us examples of what the N.T. Church was doing when he visited the various churches on his missionary journeys. Let us look at a few more texts that will shed light on the worship habits of the N.T. Church.

Saturday

↑

1. **Mt. 24:20** This is Jesus' prophetic statement about Jerusalem's fall in 70 A.D. under the Roman General, Titus. Jesus is telling Christians to still regard the Sabbath.

Sunday

← 2. **Jn. 20:19** The disciples gathered on the first day of the week (Sunday).

↑

3. **Acts 13:14** Paul and Barnabas kept the Sabbath, Saturday, at Antioch in Pisidia (fifteen years after the resurrection).

Saturday

4. **Acts 13:42** Paul and Barnabas kept the Sabbath, Saturday, preaching to Gentiles after the Jews departed (fifteen years after the resurrection).

5. **Acts 13:44** Paul and Barnabas kept the Sabbath, Saturday, by returning to preach to the whole town (fifteen years after the resurrection).

6. **Acts 16:13** Paul and his companions kept the Sabbath out in nature at Philippi, communing with God and other believers, who were also keeping the Sabbath. (It had been twenty-three years after the resurrection, and Paul still kept Saturday as the holy day.)

Sunday

7. **Acts 17:2** Paul keeps the Sabbath (Saturday) for three weeks in Thessalonica "as his manner was" (24 years after the resurrection).

8. **Acts 18:4, 11** Paul and his companions reasoned in the Synagogue, persuading Jews and Greeks **every Sabbath**. Paul stayed there for eighteen months. (Twenty-five years after the resurrection, and Paul still kept the Sabbath.)

Saturday

← (9.) **Acts 20:7** Paul and his companions met on the first day, Sunday.

Sunday ← (10.) **Rom. 14:5-6** "One man esteemeth one day above another: another esteemeth every day *alike*. Let every man be fully persuaded in his own mind...."

← (11.) **1 Cor. 16:2** Paul gave instruction for the believers to set aside an offering on the first day of the week.

The majority of the texts give support to the idea that the N.T. Church worshipped on the Sabbath, Saturday. Let us look carefully at the context of the ones that are out of line with the Big Picture.

TEXT #2 Jn. 20:19

This text is often quoted as proof for Sunday worship. But as we have already seen in our first study, there is no basis for worshipping on Sunday using this text. For a detailed look at this text and its context see Study #1, TEXT #7.

TEXT #9 Acts 20:7

This text is also frequently quoted to establish the idea for Sunday worship in the N.T. Church. As we have already seen from the study of its context, there is no basis for thinking that the N.T. Church worshipped on Sunday. For further details see Study #1, TEXT #8.

TEXT #10 **Rom. 14:5-6** "One man esteemeth one day above another: another esteemeth every day *alike*. Let every man be fully persuaded in his own mind...."

If we were going to build a doctrine on one verse of the Bible, this one would be a good place to start. This verse can be interpreted in two ways.

1. To refer to the seventh-day Sabbath (fourth commandment)

2. To refer to the Jewish ceremonial laws and holy days that were abolished at the cross

If we interpret this verse as referring to the fourth commandment, then we must carefully consider the implications of what we are saying:

1. **If** Paul is saying that you only have to keep nine out of ten of the commandments, then he is contradicting James who says if you keep "the whole law, and yet offend in one *point*, [you are] guilty of all" (James 2:10).

2. When Paul says, "Let every man be fully persuaded in his own mind," would not that make the standard of right and wrong dependent upon the opinions or impressions of the individual, rather than on the Word of God?

3. It would be saying that the details are not important to God, just as long as you follow and keep the general idea of the law. Could not we say with

Cain then, the details of this offering are not important, and I am not fully persuaded in my own mind that sacrificing a lamb is best; besides I am a farmer; I will just offer fruit (Gen. 4:2-16)

4. Paul would be saying that the law is holy, and the commandment holy, and just and good, **with a few changes**.

5. Paul would be in direct contradiction with Jesus, **if he said it does not matter** on which day you worship, because Jesus states His position in no uncertain terms, when He says, "Till heaven and earth pass, one jot [the dotting of an i in Greek] or one tittle [the crossing of a t] **shall in no wise** pass from the law, till all be fulfilled" (Mt. 5:17-18; see also Lk. 16:17).

6. It would be a contradiction of Heb. 4:4-11 where it says N.T. Christians should be keeping the Seventh-day Sabbath, as a sign of salvation by faith.

The main theme of this chapter, according to the context surrounding the verse, is that it is wrong for one person to **judge** another person, and not the Sabbath and Sunday issue (vs. 1-3, 10).

There was a controversy in the N.T. Church as to whether or not the Gentile converts had to keep the festivals and ceremonies that went with the Jewish economy (Acts 15:20, 29; 21:25). Also, part of the controversy was over whether believers should eat food that was offered to idols. (See Rom. 14:1-3 and compare 1 Cor. 8.) Paul wanted the stronger believers to stop judging the weaker ones who wanted to still observe these Jewish festivals and holidays. Even though Paul apparently got tired of running into this problem (Gal. 4:9-11), he admonished the stronger believers to be patient with the weaker. Paul was **not** saying it was all right to break one of God's commandments (the 4th) if you want, just as long as you are fully persuaded in your own mind.

TEXT #11 1 Cor. 16:2

Also frequently quoted, but the context around this verse is also just as void as the last one to give support for establishing an example of the N.T. Church worshipping on Sunday. See Study #1, TEXT #9.

SUMMARY

1. The context is judging and not Sabbath versus Sunday.

2. N.T. statements about Sabbath-keeping reflect the controversy in the early church over the Jewish ceremonial Sabbaths.

3. Paul's other statements in Romans and elsewhere reflect Paul's high regard for God's law and its unchangeable nature.

4. The implications covered earlier in Studies #1, 7, and 8 back the idea that the law does not change.

5. The Big Picture on this subject from our other studies also lend support that the law does not change.

Our final diagram would look like this:

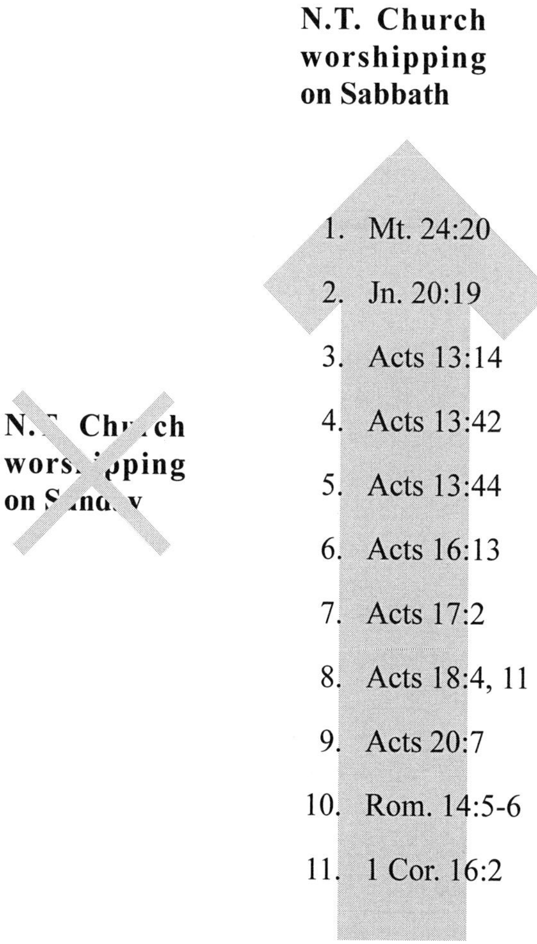

Some may say that TEXTS #3, 4, 5, 6, 7, and 8 only say that Paul went to the synagogue on Saturday because that is the day that the people were there. To this, I would quickly point out three items.

1. The purpose of the Sabbath from the creation of the world (Gen. 2:1-3), was to give man time to commune with his Maker and reflect on his relationship with God.

2. In Acts 16:13 we find Paul keeping the Sabbath **even when there was apparently no church, synagogue, or meeting place**. Paul was out in nature, communing with God, where he finds others doing the same, keeping the Sabbath holy.

3. Notice Acts 13:42 carefully. When Paul finished preaching to the people, they asked him to come back **the next Sabbath** and speak to them again. At this point, **if** Paul knew anything about a new day of worship for Christians, **namely Sunday**, he would have said, "Let us meet tomorrow," or "Let us meet next Sunday instead of on the Sabbath." **But** Paul said **no such thing** (vs. 42 and 44)! By his example and writings, **Paul kept Saturday** as his regular day of worship and taught others to do the same.

Study #6 Is Sabbath-Keeping Jewish?

If the Seventh-day Sabbath ***is*** Jewish, then it would have been abolished at the cross, with the rest of the Jewish festivals and holidays (also called Sabbaths). But **if** the Seventh-day Sabbath **is not Jewish** and for all mankind, **then** it would be for all Christians to keep, and not just for the Jews. It is true that the Hebrew people keep the Seventh-day Sabbath of the Ten Commandments and most

Christians do not. Let us look at the Big Picture on this question to find out if Sabbath-keeping is Jewish.

Seventh-day Sabbath is not Jewish but is made for all mankind; Sabbath existed long before the Jewish race existed.

Sabbath is Jewish, not for everyone.

1. **Gen. 2:1-3** At the end of the creation week God rested on the seventh day and blessed it and sanctified it.
2. **Mk. 2:27** Jesus says, "...The sabbath was made for man..." (meaning mankind, in the Greek).
3. **Jn. 8:39** The Jews claim Abraham as their father; thus their origin starts there.
4. **Heb. 4:4-11** Tells us the seventh-day Sabbath ought to be kept by the N.T. Christians as a sign of salvation by faith.

Note what other scholars have said about the Sabbath:

Martin Luther: founder of the Luthern Church

Commenting on Exodus 16:4, 22-30, Luther said, "Hence you can see that the Sabbath was before the law of Moses came and has existed from the beginning of the world. Especially have the devout, who have preserved the true faith, met together and called upon God on this day." - Translated from *Auslegung des Alten Testaments* (Commentary on the O.T.), in *Sammtliche Schriften* (Collected Writings), edited by J. G. Walch, Vol. 3, col. 950.

Moody

In regard to the Sabbath commandment Moody writes, "I honestly believe that this commandment is just as binding today as it ever was. I have talked to men who have said that it has been abrogated, but they have never been able to point to any place in the Bible where God repealed it. When Christ was on earth, He did nothing to set it aside; He freed it from the traces under which the Scribes and Pharisees had put it, and gave it its true place. 'The Sabbath was made for man and not man for the Sabbath.' It is just as practicable and necessary for men today as it ever was. - In fact, more than ever, because we live in such an intense age. The Sabbath was binding in Eden, and it has been in force ever since. This fourth commandment begins with the word 'remember,' showing that the Sabbath already existed when God wrote this law on the tables of stone at Sinai. How can men claim that this one commandment has been done away with when they will admit that the other nine are still binding?" - D.L. Moody, *Weighed and Wanting* (1898 ed.), pp. 46-47.

John Wesley: founder of the Methodist Church

"'Six days shalt thou do all manner of work. But the seventh day is the Sabbath of the Lord thy God.' It is not thine, but God's day. He claims it for His own. He always did claim it for His own, even from the beginning of the world. 'In six days the Lord made the heaven and earth, and rested the seventh day. Therefore the Lord blessed the Sabbath-day and hallowed it;' that is He made it holy; He reserved it for His own service. He appointed, that as long as the sun, or the moon, the heavens and the earth should endure, the children of men should spend this day in the worship of him who gave them life and breath and all things." - John Wesley, *A Word to a Sabbath-Breaker,* in *Works, Vol. II* (1830 ed.), pp. 164-166.

Baptist

"Jesus says: 'The Sabbath was made for man;' and the necessary influence is that from the beginning man knew the primary uses of the day, and received the benefits which it was designed to impart . . . Before the giving of the law from Sinai the obligation of the Sabbath was understood." - J. J. Taylor, *The Sabbatic Question* (Revell, 1914 ed.), pp. 20-24.

The only conclusion from this study is that the Sabbath was created by God long before there was a people called "the Jews." It is clear that the Sabbath **was** made for **all mankind** and **not just for the Jews**! The purpose of the Sabbath in the O.T. and the New is also clear. In the O.T., it was a symbol of God's creative and sanctifying power (Ex. 31:13; Eze. 20:12, 20). In the N.T., it is the same (Heb. 4:4-11) and also a sign of salvation by faith (Heb. 4:10-11).

Our final diagram in this study will look like this:

Seventh-day Sabbath is not Jewish but is made for all mankind, Sabbath existed long before the Jewish race existed.

1. Gen 2:1-3
2. Mk. 2:27
3. Jn. 8:39
4. Heb. 4:4-11
5. Bible Scholars

~~**Sabbath is Jewish, not for everyone.**~~

Study #7 Which Day is God's Sabbath Today? Can We Tell?

Today many Christians think that it is impossible to know which day is the Sabbath. They believe that the calendar has been changed many times. They say, "It is impossible to know which day is which because creation was so long ago."

First of all, let us clear the air of the "rumors of ignorance," such as, "the calendar being changed so many times that it is impossible to tell which day is which." There has been only one change in the calendar in history (1582 to be exact) when the calendar was brought into line with the movement of the planets. The Julian Calendar made provision for too many leap years, and after a long time the calendar was ten days out from the equinox (or seasons). In 1582, on October 4th, a Thursday, ten **dates** were dropped from the calendar so that the next day was Friday the 15th of October, 1582. Note the illustration below:

OCTOBER, 1582

Sun	Mon	Tues	Wed	Thurs	Fri	Sat
	1	2	3	4	15	16
17	18	19	20	21	22	23
24	25	26	27	28	29	30
31						

Notice that the weekly cycle of Sunday through Saturday was **not** disturbed. Though **dates** have changed, the days in the weekly cycle from Sunday to Saturday have never been tampered with or changed. Any good encyclopedia can be used to confirm the facts about the date 1582.

What does the Word of God say? Can we tell which day is which? Let us examine carefully the verses from Lk. 23:52 through Lk. 24:1. Notice that the context is the death, burial, and resurrection of our Lord Jesus. There are three consecutive days mentioned in the account: the preparation day (vs. 54) on which Jesus died and was buried, the Sabbath that drew on after the preparation day (Lk. 23:54, 56), and then the first day of the week (Lk. 24:1) when the disciples came to the tomb and found that Jesus was resurrected.

If we were to diagram the three days in sequence with their Biblical names and what we now call them, our chart will look like this:

Preparation Day	The Sabbath Day	1st Day of the Week
Jesus crucified and buried	Disciples rested according to the commandment	Jesus is resurrected and the tomb empty
(Lk. 23:53) *(Good) Friday*	(Lk. 23:56) *Saturday*	(Lk. 24:1-3) *Sunday*

Surely from the plain teachings of the Scripture there can be no question as to which day is which. The Sabbath is the day that came between the Preparation Day and the first day of the week. The only day between Friday and Sunday is ***Saturday***!

Review

1. The calendar was changed only once, in 1582.

2. The weekly cycle of days, Sunday through Saturday has never been changed.

3. The Biblical description of three days in a row as listed in Lk. 23:52 - 24:1 tells us which day is Sabbath.

There are several other ways to determine which day is which besides the three ways that I have already cited. They are as follows:

In many languages around the world (about 158) the root word for Saturday or the seventh day is the same as in the Bible for Sabbath (Sabbaton). No language ever confuses Saturday and Sunday by calling Sunday the Sabbath or Saturday the first day. See *A Chart of the Week* by the Rev. William Mead Jones, D.D. which was entered in the Office of the Librarian of Congress at Washington, D. C., according to an Act of Congress, in the year 1886. This chart is not exhaustive but will give any doubter assurance of the long-standing stability of the weekly cycle.

The Jewish race, though persecuted, has never lost sight of the Sabbath and which day it is. No matter what part of the world you find Jewish people today, they all worship on the same day, Saturday.

If you travel to the Holy Land, you will find at least four different religious groups with widely differing views on man's origin and how to count time. For example, Christians count time by calling this era the 1990's, meaning one thousand, nine hundred and ninety-some years after the birth of Jesus Christ or A.D.. The Jewish race, as a whole, reject this reference of keeping time, because it points to Jesus Christ as the Messiah; so they go by A.M. (Anno Mundi) or Day of the World. According to the Jewish Calendar we are now in the 5650's A.M.. There are also Moslem and Buddah worshippers in the Holy Land, and both the Moslems and Buddists have their own calendars with differing dates.

Even though there are at least four different types of worshippers in the Holy Land today, with different ways of reckoning time and keeping dates, (Christians, Jews, Moslems, and Buddists) none of these groups has confused the weekly cycle of days. Though varied in many areas of thinking, when Friday comes, **all** groups agree on Friday being Friday, Tuesday being Tuesday, etc. The weekly cycle of a seven-day week has not been altered or confused by man.

The seven-day week itself comes **not from the movement of planets, stars, or moons, but from God.** There is no logical reason why we should have a seven-day week instead of a ten-day week or something else except that God set it up with the Sabbath at the end of every week, to remind us that He created and redeemed us.

Also, people who keep Sunday rather than Saturday do not get confused and ask which day Sunday really is, do they?

We can trace the movements of days back as far as we want through astronomy to establish the lack of change in the weekly cycle of days (Sunday through Saturday). We do not have to trace the movements of days back any farther than the time of Jesus. He kept the Sabbath (Lk. 4:16), and as the Creator of the world (see the chapter on the divinity of Jesus), He knew which day was the right day for the Sabbath.

The eight ways to know for sure which day is which are listed on the following page:

Saturday = The Sabbath
No confusion on which day is which

1. Calendar changed once, 1582
2. Weekly cycle never changed
3. Days listed in Lk. 23:52 to 24:3
4. All languages call Saturday the Sabbath
5. Jews still keep Sabbath on Saturday
6. Worshippers with varied calendars in the Holy Land, but no confusion of days
7. 7 day weekly cycle, not 10
8. Study of astronomy.

~~**No way to tell which day is the Sabbath**~~

If we diagram our findings from the seven different studies on the Sabbath, we will be able to answer the original question, "Which day should we be keeping holy in the 1990's?"

Saturday is still the Sabbath;
Saturday is to be kept by N.T. Christians

	Study #1	First-Day Texts (Sunday) (plus comparison of quotes, p. 136-138)
	Study #2	Lord's Day; is it Saturday or Sunday?
Christians should worship on Sunday and keep it holy.	Study #3	The Resurrection Memorial
	Study #4	Does God's Law Change?
	Study #5	The New Testament Day of Worship
	Study #6	Is Sabbath-keeping Jewish? (plus comparison of quotes, p. 183-185)
	Study #7	Which Day is God's Sabbath Today?

Does It Really Matter?

Some might say at this point, what difference does it really make if a person worships on Saturday or Sunday? Does it really matter? We might apply that line of thinking to all of the subjects that have been covered in the book and ask, "What difference does it make what I believe, as long as I believe in Jesus Christ as my Saviour?" Does it really make any difference? There are two schools of thought on this question. **One** says it really does not matter what I believe as long as I believe in the blood of the Lamb. **The other** says it does matter what I believe, and it may very well affect my eternal destination. Which view reflects **Truth** and which view reflects **Error**?

Let us assume that God's Word does not lie and contradict itself and line up the Scripture texts to see if the Big Picture in the Bible sheds some light on this for us.

Freedom equals following Christ

↑

1. **Gen. 22:16-18** Blessings given to Abraham and promises renewed "...Because thou hast **obeyed** my voice."

Freedom is a license to sin

↑

2. **1 Sam. 15:22** "...To **obey** *is* better than sacrifice, *and* to hearken than the fat of rams."

Freedom equals following Christ

↑

(3.) **Isa. 1:19** "If ye be **willing and obedient**, ye shall eat the good of the land."

↑

(4.) **Eze. 36:26-27** "A new heart also will I give you, and a new spirit will I put within you: and I will take away the stony heart out of your flesh, and I will give you an heart of flesh. And I will put my spirit within you, and cause you to **walk** in my statutes and ye shall **keep** my judgments, and do *them*."

Freedom is a license to sin

↑

(5.) **Mt. 1:21** Jesus is a Saviour **from** sin; not a Saviour to save you **in** sin.

↑

(6.) **Mt. 7:13-14** "**Enter ye in at the strait gate**: for wide *is* the gate, and broad *is* the way, that leadeth to destruction, and many there be which go in thereat: Because strait *is* the gate, and narrow *is* the way, which leadeth unto life, and **few** there be that find it."

Freedom equals following Christ

↑

(7.) **Mt. 7:21-27** "Not every one that saith unto me, Lord, Lord, shall enter into the kingdom of heaven; but **he that doeth the will of my father** which is in heaven. Many will say..." We did "many wonderful works...then will I profess unto them, **I never knew you**: depart from me, ye that work iniquity....whosoever heareth these sayings of mine, **doeth them**, I will liken...unto a wise man..." A foolish man "heareth these sayings of mine, and **doeth them not**... great was the fall of it." (the foolish man's house)

Freedom is a license to sin

↑

(8.) **Mt. 15:3** "...**Why do ye also transgress** the commandment of God by your tradition?"

↑

(9.) **Mt. 28:19-20** "Go...teach all nations, baptizing....Teaching them **to observe** all things whatsoever I have commanded you..."

Freedom equals following Christ

↑

(10.) **Mk. 7:6-7, 9** Jesus said about the Pharisees of His day, "... This people honoreth me with *their* lips, but their heart is far from me. Howbeit **in vain do they worship me, teaching for doctrines the commandments of men**...that ye may keep your own tradition."

↑

(11.) **Lk. 24:13-27** Two disciples on the road to Emmaus were rebuked by Jesus because they didn't believe exactly what the Bible said.

Freedom is a license to sin

↑

(12.) **Jn. 14:6** "...**I am** the **way**, the **truth**, and the **life**..."

↑

(13.) **Jn. 14:15** "**If** ye love me, **keep my commandments**."

↑

(14.) **Jn. 15:14** "Ye are my friends, **if ye do** whatsoever I command you."

Freedom equals following Christ

↑

(15.) **Jn. 16:8, 13** Holy Spirit will convict the world of **sin** and of righteousness, and of judgment to come....The Holy Spirit will guide you **into truth**.

↑

(16.) **Rom. 4:20-22** Abraham did not stagger at the impossibility of **obeying God** but by faith **believed and obeyed** and it was counted to him as righteousness.

↑

Freedom is a license to sin

(17.) **Rom. 10:16** "But they have not all **obeyed** the gospel..."

↑

(18.) **2 Cor. 10:5** "Casting down imaginations, and every high thing that exalteth itself against the knowledge of God, and **bringing into captivity** every thought to the obedience of Christ."

↑

(19.) **Gal. 5:6** "For in Jesus Christ neither circumcision availeth any thing, nor uncircumcision; but faith which **worketh by love**."

Freedom equals following Christ

↑

20. **Phil. 2:8** Christ's example, "And being found in fashion as a man, he humbled himself, and became **obedient** unto death, even the death of the cross."

↑

21. **Heb. 5:8** "Though he were a Son, **yet learned he obedience** by the things which he suffered"

↑

22. **Heb. 5:9** "And being made perfect, he became the author of eternal salvation unto **all them that obey him**."

Freedom is a license to sin

↑

23. **Heb. 11:17** By faith Abraham **obeyed and was blessed**.

↑

24. **James 1:22** "But **be ye doers of the word**, and not hearers only, deceiving your own selves."

↑

25. **James 2:14, 20** "What *doth it* profit, my brethren, though a man say he hath faith, and have not works? Can faith save him?...faith **without works** is dead."

Freedom equals following Christ

↑

(26.) **James 2:21-22** "Was not Abraham our father **justified by works**, when he had offered Isaac his son upon the alter? Seest thou how **faith wrought with his works, and by works** was faith made perfect?"

↑

(27.) **James 4:17** "Therefore to him that knoweth to do good, and doeth *it* not, to him it is **sin**."

↑

Freedom is a license to sin

(28.) **1 Pet. 1:22** "Seeing ye have purified your souls in **obeying the truth** through the Spirit..."

↑

(29.) **1 Jn. 1:6** "If we say that we have fellowship with him, **and walk in darkness, we lie**, and **do not** the truth."

Freedom equals following Christ

↑

(30.) **1 Jn. 2:3-5** "And hereby we do know that we know him, **if we keep his commandments**. He that saith, I know him, and **keepeth not** his commandments, **is a liar**, and **the truth is not in him**. But whoso **keepth his word**, in him verily is the love of God perfected: hereby know we that we are in him."

Freedom is a license to sin

↑

(31.) **1 Jn. 3:22-24** "...whatsoever we ask we receive of him because we **keep his commandments**, and **do those things** that are pleasing in his

I am sure that the list I have is not exhaustive, but after careful consideration of the Big Picture we would have to draw our final diagram to look like this:

Freedom equals following Christ

1. Gen. 22:16-18
2. 1 Sam. 15:22
3. Isa. 1:19
4. Eze. 36:26-27
5. Mt. 1:21
6. Mt. 7:13, 14
7. Mt. 7:21-27
8. Mt. 15:3
9. Mt. 28:19-20
10. Mk. 7:6-7, 9
11. Lk. 24:13-27
12. Jn. 14:6
13. Jn. 14:15
14. Jn. 15:14
15. Jn. 16:8, 13
16. Rom. 4:20-22
17. Rom. 10:16
18. 2 Cor. 10:5
19. Gal. 5:6
20. Phil. 2:8
21. Heb. 5:8
22. Heb. 5:9
23. Heb. 11:17
24. James 1:22
25. James 2:14, 20
26. James 2:21, 22
27. James 4:17
28. 1 Pet. 1:22
29. 1 Jn. 1:6
30. 1 Jn. 2:3-5
31. 1 Jn. 3:22-24

Freedom is a license to sin

If you were to look hard enough, you could probably find verses in the Bible that **appear** to back up the other view, that obedience to God's commands doesn't really matter as long as one loves God. The closing scenes of this earth's history, which are upon us, Jesus likens to the days of Noah when great multitudes were being deceived and destroyed because of their own choice.

All those who stayed outside probably had good reasons for not getting in the ark. Their friends would not take that step with them. Some might have been laughed at. It just did not feel right to some. Others were probably religious in their own way but thought it ridiculous to have to get into that ark. Probably some considered the odds and chose to stay with the majority, feeling that there was safety in numbers. **It was a very small minority who chose to believe God and build the ark in the first place, let alone get in, with all those smelly animals**. One thing was certain, **the ones who followed God's instructions and were obedient to His commands were saved**. **The ones who chose not to follow God's commands, for whatever reason, good or bad, lost!**

Beliefs or correct doctrines will not save you, but **following Jesus will.** Jesus is the Word made flesh (Jn. 1:14). He will not contradict that written Word today if He Himself **is that Word.** By following the written Word you are invariably following its author, the Word made flesh, Jesus.

God will not force anyone to follow Him, but He tells us plainly that **His sheep hear His voice and follow Him** (Jn. 10:27). If you have felt the impression of the Holy Spirit guiding you toward **truth**, as you have compared Scripture with Scripture, then I would urge you to follow the prompting of the Holy Spirit **and follow the Word.**

Appendix

The Change of the Sabbath from Saturday to Sunday

Protestants, Catholics and historians agree that the change of the Sabbath, from Saturday to Sunday, comes from two sources:

1. It was officially changed in the Council of Laodicea around the date A.D. 336, by the Roman Catholic Church.

2. The change from Saturday to Sunday came about gradually as paganism and Christianity were merged under Constantine in the fourth century A.D.

Note the following quotes:

> "Sunday is a Catholic institution, and its claims to observance can be defended only on Catholic principles . . . From the beginning to the end of Scripture there is not a single passage that warrants the transfer of weekly public worship from the last day of the week to the first."
> *Catholic Press* (Sydney, Australia), Aug. 25, 1900.

"Q: Which day is the Sabbath day?
A: Saturday is the Sabbath day;
Q: Why do we observe Sunday instead of Saturday?

A: We observe Sunday instead of Saturday because the Catholic Church, in the Council of Laodicea (A.D. 336), transferred the solemnity from Saturday to Sunday."

The Rev. Peter Gelermann in *The convert's Catechism of Catholic Doctrine,* p. 50.

"The Catholic Church for over one thousand years before the existence of a Protestant, by virtue of her divine mission, changed the day from Saturday to Sunday." *Catholic Mirror,* Sept., 1893.

"Q. - Have you any other way of proving that the Church has power to institute festivals of precept?
A. - Had she not such power, she could not have done that in which all modern religionist agree with her; - she could not have substituted the observance of Sunday, the first day of the week, for the observance of Saturday the seventh day, a change for which there is no Scriptural authority." - Stephen Keena, *A Doctrinal Catechism,* 3rd Amer. Ed., rev., p. 174.

"Of course the Catholic Church claims that the change was her act...And the act is a mark of her ecclesiastical authority in religious things." H.F. Thomas, Chancellor of Cardinal Gibbons.

"The Bible says, 'Remember that thou keep holy the Sabbath day.' The Catholic Church says, 'No! By my divine power I abolish the Sabbath day and command you to keep holy the first day of the week.' And, lo, the entire civilized world bows down in reverent obedience to the command of the holy Catholic Church." Father T. Enright, C.S.R. *American Sentinel,* N.Y. June 1, 1893, p. 173.

"The observance of Sunday by the Protestants is an homage they pay, in spite of themselves, to the authority of the (Roman Catholic) church" - Monsignor Segur, *Plain Talks About the Protestantism of Today,* p. 213.

"If the Bible is the only guide for the Christian then the Seventh-day Adventist is right, in observing the Saturday with the Jew....Is it not strange, that those who make the Bible their only teacher should inconsistently follow in this matter the tradition of the Catholic Church?" *Question Box*, 1915 ed., p. 179.

For further information see the following books:

Bacchiocchi, Samuele. *From Sabbath to Sunday.* The Pontifical Gregorian University Press, Rome, 1977.

Bible Readings for the Home. Hagerstown, Md:, Review and Herald Publishing Association.

Index

Genesis

1:5 .... 129, 135
1:5, 8, 13, 19, 23, 31 132
1:14, 16-17 57
1:20 57
1:26 .... 17, 19
2:1-3 .... 141, 182, 183, 186
2:7 37
2:17 .... 23, 33, 34, 51
3:4 .... 23, 33, 34, 51
3:22 .... 17, 19
4:2-16 179
4:10 50
7:11 57
11:7 .... 17, 19
22:16-18 .... 193, 201

Exodus

3:13-14 .... 17, 19
16:4, 22-30 183
20:4-5 144
20:8-11 .... 127, 140, 141
20:11 142
20:13 144
20:15 144
20:20 142
21:5-6 111
31:13 .... 142, 185
31:18 17

Numbers

23:19 .... 2, 146, 151, 153, 154, 174

Deuteronomy

9:10 169
10:1-5 169
11:11 57
18:10-12 54
23:3 112
31:16, 27 .... 23, 33, 34, 51
31:24-26 169

1 Samuel

1:22, 28 111
1:28 111
15:22 .... 193, 201
28 53
28:6 53
28:14, 15 54
28:15 54

2 Samuel

7:12 .... 23, 33, 34, 51

1 Kings

1:21 .... 23, 33, 34, 51
2:10 .... 23, 33, 34, 51
8:30, 39 58
11:21 .... 23, 33, 34, 51
11:43 .... 24, 33, 34, 51
14:31 .... 24, 33, 34, 51
15:8 .... 24, 33, 34, 51
15:24 .... 24, 33, 34, 51
16:6 .... 24, 33, 34, 51
16:28 .... 24, 33, 34, 51
22:40 .... 24, 33, 34, 51
22:50 .... 24, 33, 34, 51

2 Kings

8:24 .... 25, 33, 34, 51
10:35 .... 25, 33, 34, 51
13:9 .... 25, 33, 34, 51
13:13 .... 25, 33, 34, 51
14:16 .... 25, 33, 34, 51
15:7 .... 25, 33, 34, 51
15:22 .... 25, 33, 34, 51
15:38 .... 25, 33, 34, 51
16:20 .... 26, 33, 34, 51
20:21 .... 26, 33, 34, 51
21:18 .... 26, 33, 34, 51
24:6 .... 26, 33, 34, 51

2 Chronicles

26:23 .... 26, 33, 34, 51
36:19 105
36:19-21 105
36:21 105

Nehemiah

9:6 16
9:6-15 .... 16, 19, 140
9:7 16
9:9-11 16
9:13 16
9:15 16

Job

7:8-10, 21 .... 26, 33, 34, 51
21:23-30 .... 26, 33, 34, 51
27:3 37
33:4 37

Psalms

6:5 .... 26, 33, 34, 40, 51
11:4 58
11:5-6 94
13:3 .... 27, 33, 34, 51
16:11 58
33:6, 9 16
37:19, 39-40 91
37:20 .... 98, 103, 105, 114
48:14 112
50:3-5 .... 70, 76, 88, 93
50:15 91
53:2 58
66:10 94
80:14 58
89:34 .... 146, 151, 153, 154, 174
91 91
102:19 58
102:27 .... 146, 151, 153, 154, 174
111:7-8 .... 146, 151, 153, 154, 174
115:17 .... 27, 33, 34, 37, 40, 51, 52
119:89 .... 146, 151, 153, 154, 174
119:105 22
139:8 58
146:4 .... 27, 33, 34, 40, 51

Proverbs

12:13 91

Ecclesiastes

9:5-6, 10 .... 27, 33, 34, 37, 40, 51
12:7 .... 27, 33, 34, 36, 37, 51

Isaiah

1:19 .... 194, 201

1:25 .... 91, 94
6:8 .... 17, 19
9:6 .... 10, 19
11:6-9 58
13:10 57
26:19 38
26:20-21 91
28:10 3
28:21 113
33:16 94
33:24 58
35:1-2 58
35:5-6 58
35:10 59
40:8 .... 146, 151, 153, 154, 174
40:31 59
47:14 .... 98, 103, 105, 114
48:10 94
51:6 .... 147, 151, 153, 154, 174
58:13 .... 140, 141
60:18 59
61:1 .... 47, 48
65:17 58
65:21-22 .... 59, 66
65:24 59
65:25 .... 59, 66
66:23 171
66:24 .... 99, 103, 104, 114

Jeremiah

6:27-29 94
17:27 105
31:15-17 .... 52, 53, 59

Ezekiel

18:4, 20 .... 27, 33, 34, 51, 99, 103, 114
20:12, 20 185
28:18 109
28:19 109
33:11 113
36:26-27 .... 194, 201

Daniel

3 91
8:8 57
12:2 .... 28, 33, 34, 51

Joel

2:30 57

Jonah

2:6 111

Micah

5:2 .... 10, 18, 19

Zechariah

8:5 59
13:9 94

Malachi

3:2-3 .... 91, 94
3:6 .... 2, 147, 151, 153, 154, 174
4:1, 3 .... 99, 103, 105, 114
4:2 .... 59, 66

Matthew

1:21 .... 194, 201
2:16-18 53
3:12 .... 99, 102, 103, 104, 114
3:16 119
5:17-18 .... 147, 151, 153, 154, 173, 174, 179
5:22, 29-30 97
7:13-14 .... 99, 103, 114, 194, 201
7:21-27 .... 195, 201
8:11 59
10:28 .... 40, 97
12:8 .... 140, 141
13:30 86
13:37-43 .... 70, 76, 93
13:39-40 .... 28, 33, 34, 35, 51, 52
15:3 .... 195, 201
16:27 .... 70, 76, 93
18:8 .... 100, 103, 104, 106, 107, 114
18:9 97
22:32 112
23:33 97
24 .... 67, 78, 83
24:4 69
24:4-5, 24 94
24:20 .... 175, 181
24:23 .... 70, 76, 93
24:23, 26 78
24:24 54
24:26 .... 70, 76, 93
24:27 .... 71, 76, 93
24:29 57
24:30 .... 71, 76, 93
24:30-31 .... 78, 88, 92
24:31 .... 71, 76, 87, 93
24:37 81
24:37-39 .... 71, 93
24:38-39 81
24:40-41 .... 71, 77, 78, 81, 83, 86, 93
24:42-44 .... 71, 77, 93

24:43 .... 77, 78, 80
24:44 78
25:31 .... 72, 76, 93
25:46 .... 100, 103, 104, 106, 107, 108, 114
26:64 .... 72, 76, 93
27:51 171
28:1 .... 129, 135
28:19 .... 18, 19, 161
28:19-20 .... 119, 195, 201

Mark

1:4 119
1:10 119
2:27 .... 183, 186
2:27-28 .... 140, 141
5:35, 39 .... 28, 33, 34, 35, 51
7:6-7, 9 .... 196, 201
9:43, 45, 47 97
9:43-44 .... 100, 103, 104, 114
12:27 112
13:21 .... 72, 76, 93
13:26-27 .... 72, 76, 93
14:62 .... 72, 76, 93
16:2 .... 129, 135
16:9 .... 129, 135
16:14 131
16:16 119

Luke

3:3 120
4:16 190
4:18 47
7:41 39
10:30 39
12:16 39
12:39 79

12:39-40 .... 73, 77
12:39-41 .... 77, 78, 79, 80, 91, 93
12:41 78
13:6 39
14:16 39
15:11 39
16:1 39
16:17 .... 147, 151, 153, 154, 173, 174, 179
16:19 39
16:19-31 .... 28, 33, 34, 35, 38, 51
16:22 39
16:22-24 40
16:23-24 40
16:26 38
16:31 39
17:23-24 .... 73, 76, 93
17:26-30 .... 73, 93
17:34-36 .... 73, 76, 77, 81, 83, 84, 86, 93
17:34-37 91
17:37 84
19:12 39
20:38 112
21:27-28 .... 73, 76, 93
23:42 42
23:43 .... 28, 33, 34, 35, 40, 41, 42, 43, 51
23:52 to 24:1 .... 187, 188, 191
23:53 188
23:54 187
23:54, 56 187
23:56 188
24:1 .... 129, 135, 187
24:1-3 188
24:13-27 .... 196, 201
24:36 131
24:36-43 .... 62, 65, 66

John

1:1-3, 10, 14 .... 10, 14, 15, 19
1:14 202

3:2 64
3:16 .... 100, 103, 114
3:23 120
3:34 161
5:17, 18 .... 10, 19
5:19, 30 13
5:28-29 .... 28, 33, 34, 35, 38, 40, 49, 51, 52
8:29 161
8:39 .... 183, 186
8:44 14
8:46 162
8:56-59 .... 11, 17, 19
10:27 202
10:30, 33 .... 11, 19
10:35 2
11:11-14 .... 29, 33, 34, 35, 49, 51
11:11-14, 23-26 38
11:23-24 .... 29, 33, 34, 35, 49, 51
11:25 53
12:34 .... 147, 151, 153, 154, 174
14:1-3 86
14:6 .... 22, 196, 201
14:15 .... 171, 196, 201
14:28 .... 11, 13, 19
15:14 .... 196, 201
16:8, 13 .... 197, 201
16:13 55
17:5 .... 11, 19
20:1 .... 129, 135
20:11-16 .... 63, 65
20:17 .... 41, 42, 43
20:19 .... 129, 130, 131, 135, 175, 177, 181
20:24-25 131
20:26-29 .... 63, 65

Acts

1:9-11 93
1:9-12 .... 74, 76
2:29, 34 .... 29, 33, 34, 35, 40, 51

2:38 .... 118, 120
2:46 133
4:10-12 .... 17, 19
4:12 140
8:13 120
8:37-39 120
13:14 .... 175, 181
13:24 121
13:36 .... 29, 33, 34, 35, 51
13:42 .... 176, 181, 182
13:42, 44 182
13:44 .... 176, 181
15:20, 29 179
16:13 .... 176, 181, 182
16:30-33 121
17:2 .... 176, 181
18:4, 11 .... 176, 181
19:4 121
19:12 43
20:6 133
20:7 .... 130, 131, 132, 135, 177, 181
20:7, 11 133
20:8 132
20:13 133
21:25 179
22:16 .... 118, 121

Romans

1:29-32 157
2:13 .... 157, 158
3:20 .... 157, 158, 160
3:23 160
3:31 .... 147, 151, 153, 154, 158, 164, 173, 174
4:15 153
4:20-22 .... 159, 197, 201
6:3-4 .... 116, 121
6:12-13 160
6:12-15 157

6:14 ... 148, 151, 152, 153, 155, 156, 159, 174
6:15 ... 160
6:18 ... 157
6:23 ... 100, 103, 112, 114, 158
7 ... 162
7:7 ... 160, 162
7:12 ... 148, 151, 153, 154, 157, 173, 174
7:13 ... 158
7:23 ... 162
8:2 ... 148, 151, 152, 153, 155, 156, 161, 162, 163, 174
8:4 ... 163
8:22-23 ... 44
10:1 ... 164
10:16 ... 197, 201
10:4 ... 148, 151, 152, 153, 155, 156, 164, 174
11:29 ... 148, 151, 153, 154, 173, 174
13:9-10 ... 158
14:1-3 ... 179
14:5-6 ... 177, 178, 181

1 Corinthians

3:13 ... 91, 94
5:7 ... 169
7:19 ... 148, 151, 153, 154, 159, 173, 174
8 ... 179
10:1-4 ... 17, 19
10:4 ... 17, 140
13:12 ... 63, 65
14:33, 40 ... 14
15:6, 20 ... 29, 33, 34, 35, 45, 51
15:20 ... 169
15:44 ... 63, 64, 65
15:50 ... 63, 65
15:51-55 ... 29, 33, 34, 35, 44, 45, 51
15:52 ... 65, 74, 87, 88, 92, 93
15:55 ... 53
16:2 ... 130, 134, 135, 177, 180, 181

2 Corinthians

5:1-8 .... 29, 33, 34, 35, 44, 45, 51
5:2 44
5:3-4 44
9:9 110
10:5 .... 159, 197, 201
11:13-14 54
12:2, 4 41
12:2-4 58

Galatians

2:21 165
3:21 165
3:24-25 .... 148, 151, 152, 153, 155, 156, 165, 174
3:25 166
4:9-11 .... 166, 180
5:6 .... 159, 197, 201
5:18 .... 149, 151, 152, 153, 155, 156, 166, 174
5:19 166
5:19-21 166
5:21 166

Ephesians

2:8-9 .... 143, 168
2:8-10 168
2:10 168
2:13 167
2:14 167
2:14, 16 167
2:15 .... 149, 151, 152, 153, 155, 156, 167, 174
2:17 167
2:18 167
3:9 .... 11, 15, 19
4:9 49
5:5 167

Philippians

1:23-24 .... 30, 33, 34, 35, 45, 51
1:24 45
2:5-8 .... 12, 13, 19
2:8 .... 198, 201
3:20 65
3:20-21 .... 61, 64, 65, 66

Colossians

1:14-16 .... 12, 13, 16, 19
1:15 14
1:16 14
2:12 .... 117, 122
2:14 168
2:14-17 .... 149, 151, 152, 153, 155, 156, 168, 174
2:17 169
3:5-6 170
3:6 .... 169, 170

1 Thessalonians

4:13-17 .... 30, 33, 34, 35, 45, 51, 52
4:15-17 44
4:16 88
4:16-17 .... 74, 76, 87, 92, 93
5:2 .... 77, 80
5:2-6 .... 74, 77, 79, 93
5:3 79
5:4 79

2 Thessalonians

1:7-10 .... 75, 76, 93, 101, 103, 106, 107, 114
1:9 86
2:8 86

1 Timothy

1:8 157
2:13 174
5:22 158
6:16 .... 30, 33, 34, 35, 45, 51

2 Timothy

2:13 .... 2, 149, 151, 153, 154, 173
2:15 .... 1, 7
3:1-5 67
4:1, 8 .... 30, 33, 34, 35, 40, 44, 45, 51, 52

Titus

1:2 .... 2, 149, 151, 153, 154, 173, 174
2:13 67

Hebrews

1:2 .... 12, 16, 19
1:6 14
4:1-3, 10 179
4:4-11 .... 142, 179, 183, 185, 186
4:9-10 143
4:10-11 185
5:8 .... 198, 201
5:9 .... 198, 201
6:18 .... 2, 149, 151, 153, 154, 173, 174
9:27 87
10:22 122
11:17 .... 198, 201
11:8-10 39
11:9-10, 16 60
13:8 .... 2, 149, 151, 153, 154, 173, 174

James

1:17 ... 2, 150, 151, 153, 154, 174
1:22 ... 198, 201
2:10 ... 144, 178
2:14, 20 ... 198, 201
2:21-22 ... 199, 201
2:26 ... 37
4:12 ... 17, 19, 140
4:17 ... 199, 201
5:1-5 ... 67

1 Peter

1:6-7 ... 91
1:22 ... 199, 201
1:25 ... 150, 151, 153, 154, 174
2:22 ... 13, 161, 162
3:18 ... 47
3:19 ... 30, 33, 34, 35, 46, 47, 48, 49, 51
3:20 ... 47
4:6 ... 31, 33, 34, 35, 46, 48, 49, 51
4:12 ... 91

2 Peter

1:20 ... 7
1:20-21 ... 3, 161
2:4 ... 97
2:4, 9 ... 31, 33, 34, 35, 51
2:6 ... 101, 103, 106, 114
3:7, 10 ... 101, 103, 106, 114
3:10 ... 75, 76, 77, 79, 80, 83, 86, 87, 91, 93

1 John

1:6 .... 199, 201
2:3-5 .... 150, 151, 153, 154, 174, 200, 201
3:2 .... 60, 61, 65, 66
3:4 .... 155, 162
3:22-24 .... 200, 201

2 John

5-6 .... 150, 151, 153, 154, 174

Jude

7 .... 101, 103, 106, 107, 114
14 89
14-15 .... 75, 76, 88, 89, 90, 93

Revelation

1:7 .... 75, 76, 86, 93
1:10 .... 139, 141
1:11 43
2:7 .... 41, 60
3:3 .... 77, 80
3:14 .... 12, 15, 19
6:9-10 .... 31, 33, 34, 35, 49, 50, 51
6:14-17 86
7:13-14 90
13:15-17 94
15:2 57
15:2-3 60
16:8-11 87
16:14 54
16:15 .... 77, 80
19:17 57
20:4 .... 31, 33, 34, 35, 49, 50, 51
20:9 .... 102, 103, 106, 114
20:9-10 108

20:10 .... 102, 103, 104, 106, 107, 108, 114
20:14 .... 102, 103, 106, 109, 114
21-22 60
21:1 58
21:2 60
21:3 60
21:4 60
21:13-21 60
21:21 60
21:23 60
21:25 61
22:1 61
22:1-2 41
22:2 61
22:5 110
22:12 .... 31, 33, 34, 35, 40, 49, 51, 52

Topical Index

ABC's of Bible study 1
Advent of Jesus 67-95
Baptism 115-123
Ceremonial law 164-172, 179-180
Divinity of Jesus 9-19
Everlasting fire 97-114
First day texts 128-139
For ever and ever 103-114
Freedom — in Christ 193-202
— in the Holy Spirit 161-164
Grace 143-161
Heaven 57-66
Holy Spirit 161-164
Law — ceremonial 164-172, 179-180
— Ten Commandment 143-174, 178-182
Obedience 161-164, 193-202
One taken and the other left 81-92
Purgatory 46-49
Rapture 67-95
Sabbath — the change of 128-139, 186-192, 203-205
— 7th day which is it? 186-192
— quotes about the 136-138, 183-185
Salvation 143-144, 150, 153-154, 160-161
Saturday 125-192
Second coming of Jesus 67-95
Second coming - signs of 67
Sprinkling 115-123
Sunday — for N.T. Christians 125-139
— quotes about 136-138, 183-185
— texts 128-139
Thief in the night 77-80
Tribulation (or time of trouble) 67-69, 88-92
Trinity 9-19
Twinkling of an eye 88-92

Abbreviations

Books of the Bible:

1 Cor. .... 1 Corinthians
1 Jn. .... 1 John
1 Ki. .... 1 Kings
1 Pet. .... 1 Peter
1 Sam. .... 1 Samuel
1 Thes. .... 1 Thessalonians
1 Tim. .... 1 Timothy
2 Chron. .... 2 Chronicles
2 Cor. .... 2 Corinthians
2 Jn. .... 2 John
2 Ki. .... 2 Kings
2 Pet. .... 2 Peter
2 Sam. .... 2 Samuel
2 Tim. .... 2 Timothy
Col. .... Colossians
Dan. .... Daniel
Deut. .... Deuteronomy
Ecc. .... Ecclesiastes
Gal. .... Galations
Gen. .... Genesis
Heb. .... Hebrews
Isa. .... Isaiah
Jer. .... Jeremiah
Jn. .... John
Lk. .... Luke
Mal. .... Malachi
Mk. .... Mark
Mt. .... Matthew
Neh. .... Nehemiah
Num. .... Numbers
Phil. .... Philippians
Prov. .... Proverbs
Psm. .... Psalms
Rev. .... Revelation
Rom. .... Romans
Zech. .... Zechariah

Others:

N.T. .... New Testament
O.T. .... Old Testament
Vs. .... verse or verses